A BADGER BOY IN BLUE

A BADGER BOY IN BLUE
THE CIVIL WAR LETTERS OF CHAUNCEY H. COOKE

*With an Introduction and Appendix
by William H. Mulligan, Jr.*

Wayne State University Press Detroit

© 2007 by Wayne State University Press, Detroit, Michigan 48201. All rights reserved.
No part of this book may be reproduced without formal permission.

11 10 09 08 07   5 4 3 2 1

Library of Congress Cataloging-in-Publication Data

Cooke, Chauncey H. (Chauncey Herbert), 1846–1919.
 A badger boy in blue : the Civil War letters of Chauncey H. Cooke / with an introduction and appendix by William H. Mulligan, Jr.
   p. cm.
 ISBN-13: 978-0-8143-3343-3 (pbk. : alk. paper)
 ISBN-10: 0-8143-3343-5 (pbk. : alk. paper)
 1. Cooke, Chauncey H. (Chauncey Herbert), 1846–1919—Correspondence. 2. United States. Army. Wisconsin Infantry Regiment, 25th (1862–1865) 3. Soldiers—Wisconsin—Correspondence. 4. United States—History—Civil War, 1861–1865—Personal narratives. 5. Wisconsin—History—Civil War, 1861–1865—Personal narratives. 6. United States—History—Civil War, 1861–1865—Campaigns. I. Mulligan, William H. II. Title.

E537.525th .C476 2007
973.7'475092—dc22
2006038135

Chauncey H. Cooke's letters were originally printed in *Wisconsin Magazine of History*, 1920–22.

∞ The paper used in this publication meets the minimum requirements
of the American National Standard for Information Sciences—Permanence of Paper
for Printed Library Materials, ANSI Z39.48-1984.

CONTENTS

Introduction vii
William H. Mulligan, Jr.

Preface to *Wisconsin Magazine of History* edition 1

Off to War 5

Life at Old Camp Randall 27

Into the Southland 37

The Vicksburg Campaign 59

The Atlanta Campaign 83

Appendix: Biographical Sketches 117

INTRODUCTION

William H. Mulligan, Jr.

In a heavily wooded family cemetery along Cooke's Farm Road outside Gilmanton, Buffalo County, in western Wisconsin, a reddish granite tombstone proudly summarizes the life of Chauncey H. Cooke.

> COOKE
> Chauncey H.
> 1846–1919
> A Soldier of the Civil War for
> the Union of the States and
> Freedom of the Slaves.
> A Friend of the Colored Races
> The Indian and The Negro.

Clearly, Chauncey H. Cooke was proud of his military service during the Civil War and his role in ending slavery. Later in his life he periodically published the letters he had written home during the war in the Mondovi *Herald,* one of the local newspapers, and other letters on his experiences as a pioneer settler in the county. The letters later appeared as a small, very limited edition book. Shortly after his death in May 1919, the letters appeared serially in the *Wisconsin Magazine of History* with some annotations.[1] Unfortunately, Cooke's original letters have long since been lost. Because Cooke himself acknowledged that he had changed the letters, we do not know just what the published letters represent. Are they the views of an idealistic teenager who marched off to preserve the Union and end the evil of slavery, or are they those of an older, wiser man reflecting on the great adventure of his youth and its success in ending slavery? The preface to the letters in the *Wisconsin Magazine of History* includes a statement from Cooke about his changes:

I am frank to admit that the printed letters are not a verbatim copy of the originals, if in any degree their fidelity be questioned. Where the lead was poor and letters illegible I had to improvise, or where I had sinned to excess in spelling and grammar I made amendments. And in narration of fact or situation which seemed obscure or indefinite I substituted more specific language. In matter the printed letters are absolutely true to the originals. I invented no facts nor situations.[2]

Internal evidence in the letters suggests that the changes Cooke made were somewhat more substantial than he indicates in a number of instances. The "more specific language" occasionally includes information about troop movements and events that Cooke could not have known when he was writing the letters. For example, when Cooke writes on March 25, 1863, "Grant has driven Gen. Pemberton into Vicksburg and is closing in around that city," the events had not yet happened. Similarly, Cooke's statement to his mother on August 4, 1864, that if Atlanta falls "we can march to the sea and then goodbye to the rebellion" anticipates events by several months. Cooke could not have known of a planned march to the sea at the time. Other specific examples also suggest revision more substantial than what Cooke indicated. And it is reasonable to assume that he made still other changes to reflect his more mature views on various subjects, including race, or changes in his attitude as a result of events that followed the war. He never claimed otherwise. Without the original letters to compare, it is impossible to know with any certainty which passages represent the reactions of the young Union soldier and which represent the mature Wisconsin farmer, but it may not be critical. Cooke's letters maintain a great deal of his youthful enthusiasm as he marched off to war. They also give us his reflections on that experience and offer us a useful and interesting window into the Civil War and the motivations of the men who fought it. Chauncey Cooke's vantage point on the war is both interesting and valuable.

There can be little doubt about the sincerity of Cooke's opposition to slavery as young man while he served in the army. His father and family generally were outspoken opponents of slavery in the decades leading up to the Civil War, and Chauncey appears to have shared those attitudes. In one local debate over slavery, Samuel Cooke clinched his argument by saying, "I have a boy who wants to go to war and I would give his life as cheerfully as Abraham offered his son if necessary that the slaves might be freed."[3] Chauncey later recalled, "Father meant all right, though it seemed hard, but I love him all the more for it, although I suppose I am the boy he meant for the sacrifice."[4] Following the war, he enrolled at what is now the University of Wisconsin–La Crosse and trained as a teacher. He then taught for a number of years in Freedmen's schools in Texas before returning home to Buffalo County to farm for the rest of his life.[5] His tombstone inscription tells us what he thought was important about that life and his service in the army.

Chauncey H. Cooke was born in Columbus, Ohio, in 1846. His family was among the pioneer settlers of Buffalo County. Samuel Shattuck Cooke moved his wife and two young sons there from Winchester, Indiana, in 1856 to take up land he had scouted on an earlier trip. Both Chauncey and his younger brother, Warren, published descriptions of the trip west in a covered wagon and on establishing a farm and a life on the Wisconsin frontier.[6] The Cooke family lived much as other pioneer families did, clearing land; planting and harvesting crops; hunting deer, elk, and bear for meat; trapping beaver and other animals for fur and a little cash. Indians occasionally camped near the Cookes' farm, and while there was little interaction, Warren Cooke reported, "They were quiet and civil in all ways."[7] The family's other contacts with Indians were also peaceful and positive.

In August 1862 Chauncey Cooke joined a number of other young men from Gilmanton and around Buffalo County and signed on for three years in the Union army with the 25th Wisconsin Volunteer Infantry. He was underage at sixteen and worried that the mustering officer would catch him and send him home (as he describes in his letter of September 15, 1862), but he was not and he served until nearly the end of the war when illness led to an early discharge on May 15, 1865.[8] He missed marching with the 25th in the Grand Review in Washington by a few days and their welcomes home at Milwaukee and Madison, where the regiment formally disbanded on June 11, 1865.[9]

There is little doubt why Cooke enlisted. His father was a staunch abolitionist, and young Cooke, too, was an abolitionist who enlisted to end slavery. His unit, however, was first sent to Minnesota to suppress an Indian uprising. This troubled Cooke for two reasons, as he reports in his letters home—he had enlisted in the army to fight to end slavery and he thought the Indians had been mistreated and had legitimate grievances against the government.

As with most Civil War units, men already known in the local community recruited the unit and served as its regimental officers. Col. Milton Montgomery and Lt. Col. (initially major) Jeremiah M. Rusk both were well known in the area, as were the other regimental and company officers. Both Montgomery and Rusk won brevets (temporary rank) as brigadier generals for their distinguished service during the war. Rusk later served as governor of Wisconsin and as secretary of agriculture in the Benjamin Harrison administration.[10]

The 25th was organized in La Crosse, Wisconsin, at Camp Salomon, named for Wisconsin's governor. Chauncey enlisted in Company G with seven others from Gilmanton, including John W. McKay, who served as second lieutenant. All but one of the Gilmanton men made it safely through the war; John W. Christian was killed in action at Decatur, Georgia. Another Gilmanton man, John F. Brobst, also wrote letters home—to a young woman he married after the war—and his letters give us a second glimpse into the service of the 25th and some information about Chauncey.[11] Brobst, Cooke, and Brobst's future wife had been friends before the war.

The 25th would become an active, fighting unit. However, within days of being mustered into Federal service in September 1862 it was sent, not south to fight the Rebels, but northwest to help deal with a potential Indian uprising that was causing a great deal of concern among settlers in Minnesota. The regiment, which was headquartered at New Ulm, dispersed across a wide area but saw no action, as the threat evaporated without incident.

The regiment's service in Minnesota ended in late November, and its men endured a difficult two-week march overland to Winona, Minnesota, where the soldiers boarded riverboats for La Crosse and finally a train for Camp Randall in Madison. Two months later they finally received orders to head south for Cairo, Illinois. They arrived in Cairo on February 19, 1863, only two days after leaving Wisconsin. The next day they went on to Columbus, Kentucky, one of the major staging areas for Grant's Vicksburg campaign, as part of the 16th Army Corps under Gen. Stephen A. Hurlburt. On April 27 the 25th was dispatched to help defend Cape Girardeau, Missouri, but the unit was delayed by harassing Rebel forces and arrived after the battle was over. Cooke and his fellows returned to garrison duty at Columbus until the end of May.

While at Columbus, Cooke found much to write about, especially his encounters with former slaves. Like many Northern abolitionists, he had had no prior contact with slaves or African Americans. He was impressed with the intelligence and general demeanor of the contrabands (as the former slaves were known). He was especially impressed when he met former slaves from Louisiana who spoke both French and English. Although Cooke was liberal in his views on race by the standards of the 1860s, his language will sound harsh and bigoted to readers today. It is symptomatic of how deeply ingrained attitudes of white superiority were. What also comes across is how important Harriet Beecher Stowe's novel *Uncle Tom's Cabin* was in shaping Northerners' ideas about slavery and African Americans. A number of Cooke's letters from Columbus refer to the novel. In his letter of March 5, 1863, and in others he matched former slaves he encountered with characters in the novel.

The 25th was not destined to spend the war on garrison duty, and in May 1863 it headed south to join the Vicksburg campaign, reassigned to a new brigade known as Montgomery's Brigade, commanded by their own Colonel Montgomery. While stationed at Snyders Bluff, Mississippi, they erected fortifications but had major problems with illness—at one point five hundred were sick and only one hundred were fit for duty. The 25th next found itself in Arkansas, where it remained from July 1863 to late January 1864, when Montgomery commanded the District of Eastern Arkansas. This too was largely a period of garrison duty. No letters survive from this period. Early in 1864, the unit, now commanded by Jeremiah Rusk, went with Sherman on his expedition to Meridian, Mississippi.

In March the 25th was reassigned to Chattanooga, the new center of action in the western theater, and went back to Cairo and then up the Tennessee River to Crumps Landing, Alabama, and then overland through Florence, Athens; and Mooresville to Decatur, Alabama. It engaged the Confederates at Decatur on April 7, the first time the unit saw actual combat. After a month at Decatur the 25th entered a period of sustained action as they moved by rail to Chattanooga to rejoin the 16th Corps, now commanded by Gen. Grenville M. Dodge, and the Atlanta campaign. The 25th saw action at Resaca, Dallas, Kennesaw Mountain, Decatur, and, finally, Atlanta. At Decatur, Colonel Montgomery, who had rejoined the unit, was wounded and captured. The unit then headed for the coast as part of Sherman's March to the Sea. Once that campaign ended, the 25th went by ship to South Carolina and fought in a number of engagements until the end of the war. It was one of the units present when Gen. Joseph

Johnston surrendered the last Confederate army east of the Mississippi on April 26, 1865.

Cooke did not witness all of this firsthand. He was in a field hospital in Marietta, Georgia, by August 4, 1864, and wrote the last surviving letter on August 20. The 25th was among the units that marched in the Grand Review in Washington, D.C., and formally mustered out of service on June 7. It returned to Milwaukee and then Madison, where the unit officially disbanded.[12]

The original strength of the 25th was 1,018 men. Just over four hundred had joined the unit during the war as replacements, most in 1864 when the unit engaged in the most combat. When the unit mustered out it had 722 on active duty. It had lost 422 men to disease and combat, 165—like Cooke—had already been discharged for various reasons, usually illness or injury. Sixty-five had transferred to other units, and 20 had deserted. Its losses, exactly 50 percent, were close to the norm for Federal units and the highest for any Wisconsin unit.

The experience of the 25th covers pretty much the full range of experiences for Civil War units. Assembling and training near home at Camp Salomon in La Crosse, garrison duty at Columbus, Kentucky, occupation of conquered territory in Arkansas, and combat both in major battles and as part of campaigns—in their case major campaigns such as Vicksburg, Atlanta, and Sherman's March to the Sea—the men dealt with death and disease in camp and losses in combat. They shared in the victory parade in Washington and then returned home to resume their lives.

We see all of this through the eyes of a bright, perceptive young man who had joined the army for a clear purpose. At the end of a long life, he remained proud of that service and its results.

Notes

1. "A Badger Boy in Blue: The Letters of Chauncey H. Cooke," *Wisconsin Magazine of History* 4 (1920–21): 75–100, 207–17, 322–44, 431–56; 5 (1921–22): 63–98.

2. "A Badger Boy in Blue" (1920–21): 76–77. The editor of the *Wisconsin Magazine* also corrected "a few instances of obvious mistakes in printing and certain crudities of punctuation or other typographical style" (77).

3. James I. Clarke, *The Civil War of Private Cooke: A Wisconsin Boy in the Union Army* (Madison: State Historical Society of Wisconsin, 1955), 1.

4. Ibid.

5. Ibid., 11.

6. Chauncey H. Cooke, "A Pioneer Boyhood," in Franklyn Curtiss-Wedge, comp., *History of Buffalo and Pepin Counties, Wisconsin*, vol. 2 (Winona, MN: H. C. Cooper, Jr., 1919), 951–57. A longer and richer account appears in Warren W. Cooke, "A Frontiersman in Northwestern Wisconsin," *Wisconsin Magazine of History* 23 (1939–40): 281–303, 406–26.

7. W. Cooke, "Frontiersman," 290.

8. While Lee's surrender at Appomattox Courthouse on April 9, 1865, is now considered the end of the Civil War, there were several Confederate armies in the field at the time and it was several months before all had surrendered.

9. *Roster of Wisconsin Volunteers in the War of the Rebellion, 1861–1865*, 2 vols. (Madison: Democrat Printing, 1886), 2:282.

10. Henry Casson, *"Uncle Jerry": Life of General Jeremiah M. Rusk: Stage Driver, Farmer, Soldier, Legislator, Governor, Cabinet Officer* (Madison, WI: Junius W. Hill, 1895).

11. Margaret B. Roth, ed., *"Well, Mary": Civil War Letters of a Wisconsin Volunteer* (Madison: University of Wisconsin Press, 1960).

12. The service of the 25th is summarized in William DeLoss Love, *Wisconsin in the War of the Rebellion; A History of All Regiments and Batteries* (Chicago: Church and Goodman, 1866), 996–98, and discussed more fully in E. B. Quinn, *The Military History of Wisconsin* (Chicago: Clarke and Co., 1866), 734–45.

PREFACE TO *WISCONSIN MAGAZINE OF HISTORY* EDITION

"Old men for counsel, young men for war," runs the ancient proverb. The men who saved the Union in the sixties were for the most part young men, thousands of them being "boys in blue" literally as well as figuratively. Living in the town of Dover, Buffalo County, on the raw Wisconsin frontier when the Civil War broke out was a clumsy, overgrown boy named Chauncey H. Cooke. Born at Columbus, Ohio, in May, 1846, he had grown up in the Wisconsin wilderness; sleeping by night under the shake shingle roof of a rude log house through which in winter the snow sifted freely down upon him; by day, when not engaged in the hard toil of the frontier farm, hunting deer and bear and wild fowl or fraternizing with the red children of the forest who still sojourned in this region. It is not strange that such a course of life developed in him a "constitution like a horse," and a physical stature beyond his years. When the call to arms came in the summer of 1861 young Cooke, although barely turned fifteen, was eager to respond to it. The next season came the Sioux troubles in Minnesota, and therewith the famous panic on the part of the people of Wisconsin which constitutes perhaps the most curious psychological episode in our history. But already our Buffalo County lad, having reached the mature age of sixteen, had resolved to enlist, even though to accomplish this might necessitate the stultification of his puritan training to the extent of telling the mustering officer a lie about his age. Going down to La Crosse for this purpose in September, 1862, he was enrolled in Company G, Twenty-fifth Wisconsin Infantry, and shortly thereafter, instead of being sent to Dixie, was on his way northward to share in the campaign of General Pope against the Sioux of Minnesota. The young soldier saw no fighting in this campaign. However, he made his first contact with the life of the great world outside the secluded valley in which he had passed his boyhood hitherto; and his letters home during this period present both an unusual view of the Indian trouble and the charmingly fresh and unsophisticated narrative of the reactions of the pioneer boy of puritan antecedents to the environment in which he found himself. With the passing years came a greater degree of sophistication, but essentially a boy our subject remained when in May, 1865, on his nineteenth birthday he was mustered out of the service after nearly three years' campaigning.

The letters which we print require but little editing. Since the originals are no longer in existence, however, it is in order here to tell the pedigree of the copies we present for the enjoyment of our readers. Mr. Cooke died at his home in Mondovi in May, 1919. The character of citizen he was is perhaps sufficiently indicated by the fact that by common consent the business houses of the city closed for two hours on the day of his funeral. A few years earlier these letters had been printed in the Mondovi *Herald*, and fifty copies of the entire collection were struck off in crude booklet form with the title, "Soldier Boy's Letters to his Father and Mother, 1862–65." A copy of this booklet came into the hands of the present editor, and struck by the character of its contents he took up with Mr. Cooke, a few months before his death, the question of reprinting the letters in this magazine. To this end a request was made for the loan of the original letters and this evoked the explanation from their author that most of them had been destroyed or given away to various friends. "Many of them," he continued, "were scrappy and illegible to anyone save myself, written on all sorts of paper and nearly all in pencil. The soldier's portfolio case for carrying paper and pen and ink, usually a part of his equipment while in training quarters, was nearly always thrown away when real service on the march began. I think you will find an agreement among the old vets that any chance bit of paper picked up from rifled country stores or dwellings along the line of march was the source of supply for letter paper much of the time. I am frank to admit that the printed letters are not a verbatim copy of the originals, if in any degree their fidelity be questioned. Where the lead was poor and letters illegible I had to improvise, or where I had sinned to excess in spelling and grammar I made amendments. And in narration of fact or situation which seemed obscure or indefinite I substituted more specific language. In matter the printed letters are absolutely true to the originals. I invented no facts nor situations."

With such a history, then, we take the letters from the booklet in question. But since the printer thereof apologizes for "errors of omission and commission" on the part of the proof reader, and since in any event the copies do not purport to be exact reproductions of the originals, we have deemed it the part of good judgment to eliminate from the copies a few instances of obvious mistakes in printing and certain crudities of punctuation or other typographical style, for which the printer rather than the author was probably usually responsible.

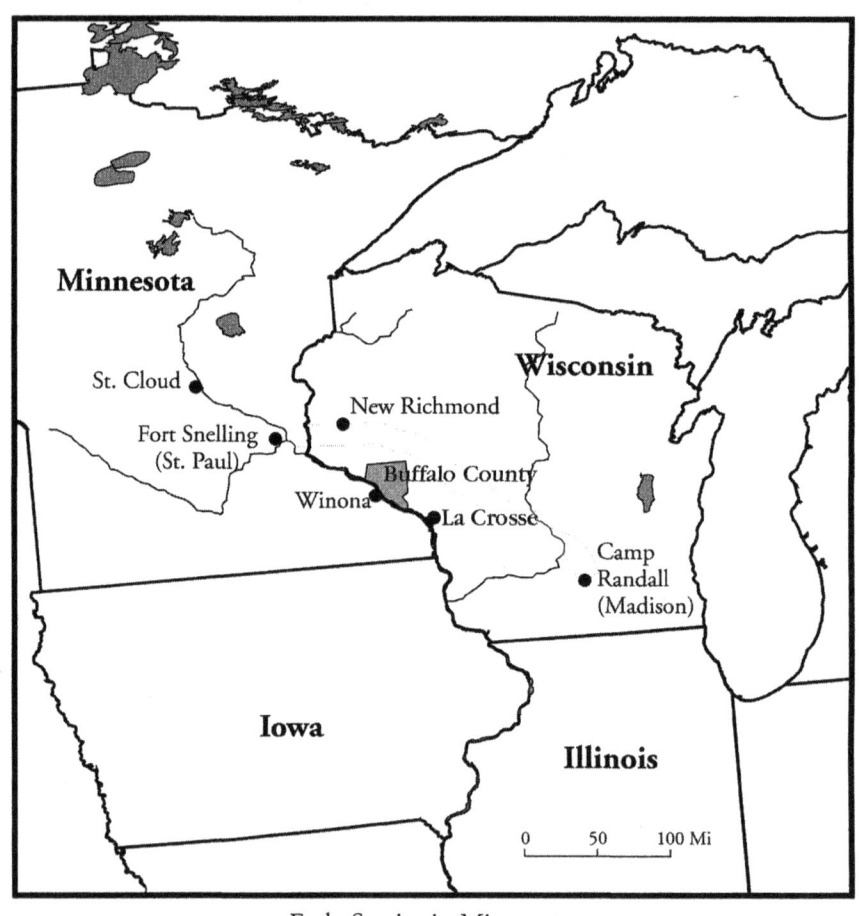

Early Service in Minnesota.
September 1862–February 1863

OFF TO WAR

Camp Soloman, La Crosse, Wis.,
Hd. Quarters 25th Wis. Vol. Inft.
Sept. 15th, 1862.

Dear Parents:

I am sitting on the straw in my tent with my paper on a trunk for a desk, this is Monday, before breakfast that I am writing you. This has been a very busy week for the soldiers.

We did not get through mustering until last evening which as you know was Sunday. The mustering officer was here all day, and he was a fierce looking fellow. Anyhow that's the way he looked to us younger boys that couldn't swear we was 18. We had to muster in all the same, if it was Sunday. Some of the boys tho't it was a bad omen, and meant bad luck. We were not exactly mustered in because we did not get our pay, but the companies were drawn up in line, one at a time, and the officer with his hands behind his back walked along ten feet or so in front of the line looking every man in the face. Every one he suspicioned of being under 18, he would ask his age. He turned out a lot of them that were not quite 18. Some of them that might have been old enough, were getting homesick and was glad to get out of it by fibbing a little. Seeing how it was working out with the rest, I did not know what to do. I went to see our captain but he said he could not help me. He said his interceding would do no good. I saw our Chaplain and he told me to tell the truth, that I was a little past 16, and he tho't that when the mustering officer saw my whiskers he would not ask my age. That is what the boys all told me but I was afraid. I had about made up my mind to tell him I was going on 19 years, but thank heaven I did not have a chance to lie. He did not ask my age. I am all right and the boys were right. Say do you know the sweat was running down my legs into my boots, when that fellow came down the line, and I was looking hard at the ground fifteen paces in front.

I suppose I am a full fledged soldier now. I have got my uniform and that awful mustering officer has gone. While I am writing, the fife and drums are playing again; how I wish you could come down and see the soldiers. To see a thousand soldiers on regimental drill or parade is what visitors call a splendid sight. Hundreds of people in La Crosse come out to see us every evening. There was about five hundred visitors here last night to see us on dress parade. Gen. Pope[1] got off here last Saturday evening and we expected to see him in camp but he did not come. I was in town the evening he came but my pass did not last long enough to see the General. But I saw some of his aids. Chester Ide's wife came from Mondovi yesterday. There is hundreds of other things I could speak of but I don't have paper or time to mention them. But there is one more thing I have to tell you, we are to start for Cincinnatti next Thursday, so if you can come down before that time you will find me here.

We are to get our money tomorrow and if we do I will get my picture taken. We got our guns yesterday. If you write at once, direct to La Crosse Wisconsin.

Your loving son,
Chauncey.

P.S. The boys that were rejected lit out last night and took their uniforms with them.

HEADQUARTERS, 25TH WISC.
LA CROSSE, WIS., SEPT. 20, 1862.

Dear Parents:

One more week has gone and we are still in La Crosse. Our daily stunt is to drill four hours a day. Our drillmaster is a nice little fellow. He has been

---

1. General John Pope was a native of Kentucky who graduated at West Point in 1842 and served continuously in the regular army until his retirement in 1886. In the year 1861 and the early part of 1862 he attracted much favorable attention by his successful operations against the Confederate forces in Missouri. As a consequence he was summoned to Washington at the end of June and given command of the Army of Virginia, where in a period of several weeks of strenuous fighting he proved unequal to the task of coping with such opponents as Lee and Jackson and asked to be relieved of the command. He was now assigned to the Department of the Northwest, and under his general superintendence the Sioux uprising was put down, although the actual work had been largely done before Pope's arrival by state volunteers under the command of Henry H. Sibley. Pope was an implacable foe of the Indians and desired to have several hundred of the captured Sioux executed under court-martial proceedings. Fortunately President Lincoln interposed; due to this interference the number actually executed was reduced to thirty-eight. A recent historian of Minnesota observes that the fate accorded those who escaped execution was scarcely more enviable than that of the thirty-eight who were hanged. [*Wisconsin Magazine of History*]

sent to us to drill us and will be made our 2nd lieutenant. He is a proud bugger in his brand new suit of blue with gold cord on his legs and shoulder straps and he walks so darn straight he leans backward. But he's a good one.

There is not a man but would be too glad if we had orders to march for Dixie tomorrow. It's awful tiresome staying here doing nothing. It's harder work than farming. The Governor telegraphed to the Colonel of the regiment yesterday that we were liable to get orders to go up the river to Fort Snelling by boat and sent into the Sioux Indian country. There is a boy 14 years old here in camp, who came from above St. Paul, whose father was murdered by the Indians ten rods from him last week. The boy escaped by crawling under a bridge and waiting till a team came along. He came to St. Paul and worked his way down on a steamboat to this place.

I haven't been homesick a minute. I like drilling pretty well and our Bob, that is the name of our lieutenant, says we step up like regulars. Please excuse these short letters. Tell George Wooster to write and I will answer him. Also tell sister Do to add a line when you write.

Is she catching any fish these days? I hope trapping will be good this fall so father can make a little extra change. Are the pigeons in the stubble like they were last fall when I shot 19 at one crack? My goodness, how I would like a pigeon pot pie. Tell father he will find a lot of shot in the old leather knife case on that shelf in the entry way. They are some I bought last year when Fred Rosman and I were going to get rich shooting prairie chickens and selling them to the steamboats. I wish we could get our money so I could come home a few days. I suppose you got my picture. How do I look as a soldier? I tell you it looks military like to see the fellows in their regulation blue.

Write often as you can conveniently, anything from home seems good.

Chauncey.

P.S. I have reopened this letter to say we have orders to report at once to St. Paul. I think we will start in the morning. Don't write till I can give you my address.

La Crosse, Wis., Sept. 21, 1862.

Dear Mother:

I wrote you yesterday we had orders to report to St. Paul to fight the Sioux Indians, in Minnesota. Sure enough we are packing things and will leave here in the morning on the big sidewheel steamer *St. Paul* for up river. Some of the boys are mad and some are glad. Some say they did not enlist to fight Indians but to fight rebels, but military orders must be obeyed. If I thought the young Sioux chief who has been to our place so many times with his hunting party who was so good to us, letting us have elk meat and venison for a little of nothing, I should not like to think of shooting at them. I remember father said, if a few Indian contractors were scalped, there would be no trouble. I read last night in the paper a letter from Bishop Whipple of Minnesota, who said the government had not kept its promise with the Indians, that they had no blankets and no rations of beef, and that was the reason they went on the warpath. The bow and arrows the chief's son gave me, I wish you would see that they are not lost. I don't believe Indian John stole Mr. Cripp's gun. He is a good Indian and if he is not killed in the war he will bring it back.

I will finish this in the morning.

Sept. 21st. I am sitting on the hurricane deck of the *St. Paul* steamer where our Company has been assigned for the trip to Fort Snelling. We were an hour filing on board the boat this morning. Everybody is feeling good. Some of them are happier than they ought to be. Bill Anderson and some of the Mondovi boys are pretty well loaded. Chet Ide doesn't drink, but he is laughing louder at the fellows who do drink. Gile Bump of Mondovi and I crawled under the ledge over the cabin to get in the shade. The boat has an awful load.

A thousand men with all the fixtures and equipment. There is not room to lie down! The band is kept pretty busy. Whenever we pass a boat or reach a town the band pounds and blows for all it's worth. The women and girls wave their handkerchiefs, and every fellow thinks it's meant for him. I'll bet there never was so jolly a crew on this boat before. When the boat stopped at Winona some of the boys took a high dive from the top of the wheelhouse into the river. I never thought they would come up again but they did, and swam back to the yawl and climbed into that and were pulled up by ropes onto the boiler deck. We have just passed Fountain City and I must close this letter so as to mail it at Alma. The boat stops at every town, but no soldier is allowed to step off the boat. We have just passed a raft and the way the logs teeter in the waves is a wonder. The fellows shake their fists and yell dirty, hoodlum stuff, but the boys in blue give it back to them in plenty.

Tell Elder Morse's folks that Henry is well and spoiling for a fight.

Chauncey.

Dear Mother.—

I missed the Alma boat and so I'll add a few lines more. We reached St. Paul and everybody was on the shore to greet us. They are mighty glad to have soldiers come as the Indians are gathering in big forces, and there may be bloody times. After waiting for orders we steamed on to Fort Snelling six miles above, and after landing in the bushes at the mouth of the Minnesota River, we climbed the high bluff where the Fort is located. They call this fort the American Gibraltar, if you can guess the meaning, steep wall nearly around it, and some big black cannons pointing in all directions.

I tell you those cannons have a wicked look. They are the first I have ever seen. I have just discovered I have a two-dollar counterfeit bill, so I am on half rations for money. We got our knapsacks this evening, and expect to start up the Minnesota and Mississippi Rivers to hunt Indians in a day or two.

Wish you would make me a pair of two fingered mittens, it would save me $1.50; make them out of thin buckskin. There is a lot of buck Indians in the stone jail of the fort, who are guarded. They are some of the ringleaders, who incited the massacre. One of them looks just like One Eye, who staid around our place so much.

Chauncey.

Direct to Co. G., Ft. Snelling.

St. Cloud, Minn., Oct. 2, 1862.
Co. G. 25th Regt.

Dear Parents:

In my last I wrote you of our arrival at Fort Snelling and that we were to march into the Indian Country in a day or two. Fort Snelling is a fine place and I hadn't got tired of it when orders came to divide our Regiment, the right wing to go up the Minnesota River and the left wing up the Mississippi. Our Co. is in the left wing so we came up the Mississippi River. The first night after quitting Ft. Snelling we camped in the edge of Minneapolis, a pretty town at the Falls of St. Anthony. St. Anthony, just across the river, has some nice big buildings and is the biggest place. It was awfully hot the day we left the fort and our extra blankets and belts full of ammunition made a load. But we felt good and after supper I scuffled with Casper Meuli and Max Brill till bed time. I know father advised me not to do any wrestling, but a fellow can't say no all the time. A lot of us rolled up in our blankets under the trees on the bank of a creek with no tents that night. A lot of women or girls from town came into camp and walked over us as if we were logs. I thot they were pretty fresh. Some of the older soldiers talked pretty plain to them but they didn't seem to care. After awhile they were ordered away and then we went to sleep. The next night and the night after I slept in barns on the hay. The people seemed to be Germans but they were good and gave us all they had of milk and bread. The boys would gather like pigs round a milk pan, three or four drinking at the same time. We came into St. Cloud last night. We crossed the Mississippi here. It isn't the mighty stream here that it is at Alma, I could throw a stone across and hit a dog up here. These people gave us a warm welcome. Some of our boys came down with the measles and will go into hospital quarters until they get well. I have a queer sort of feeling, perhaps its measles with me. You know I never was sick. When the surgeon examined me in La Crosse he hit me a slap and told me I had a constitution like a horse. I told him my living for some years had been buck meat, beaver's tails and bear flesh. He said, "You are a tough one, that is plain to see." I am sitting on a big rock on the bank of the Mississippi. It seems strange that this clear, beautiful stream is the same yellow, broad river that runs so near my home. As I write I am using a fine-tooth comb and I am finding bugs. I don't know where I got them, but I've got them. I was ashamed to be seen combing in camp so I came down behind the big rocks by the river. The other boys must have them. No Indians yet. The old settlers tell us the buffaloes were here but a few years ago. I have seen some of their horns, sharp, black wicked things. Their trails can be seen on the prairies and along the river banks. I remember father saying the buffaloes and Indians would disappear about the same time. Pot hunters would slay the buffaloes for their skins, and the white man's whiskey was as surely slaying the Indian. Tomorrow we take up our march to Richmond, twenty miles away. I will write you then.

Your son
Chauncey.

P.S. Tell father not to brag so much on Webster as a speller. I know I am not in his class quite, but I have bought me a pocket dictionary and I am studying it every day. Our Chaplain came along last night and saw me with it. He stopped and looked at it; well, he said it is next thing to a testament anyhow.

Good bye.

St. Cloud Hospital, St. Cloud, Minn.
Oct. 20th, 1862.

Dear Mother, Father, and All the Rest.

I am writing you from a sick bed propped up on the back of a chair made soft with pillows. You must think it strange that you have got no letters these three weeks but if you knew how fearfully sick I have been you would understand. I have been a mighty sick boy with the measles all this time in a big room in the city building along with ten other of my comrades. Three others of my Co. are here. Andy Adams, one of my chums from Mondovi, is one of them and he has been very sick. I tell you mother it is a terrible thing to be sick among strangers anyway. I've tho't of home and you so many times. Maybe if I had ever been sick before it would not have seemed so bad, but I want to tell you my dear mother, I never want to be sick away from you. The women of the town came in every day to give nice things to eat and make lemonade for us but they were all strange and new ones came nearly every day. They were kind, of course but O, I don't know. I felt if they were thinking more of their nice clothes and how fine they looked than of us. They wouldn't give me all the water I wanted, and I was always so thirsty. I just dreamed all the time. I don't want to talk like a baby, mother, and the boys say, "Don't write any bad news to your father and mother," but you have always told me I should tell the truth and I believe its all right. God knows I never felt before what it meant to have a good home and a kind father and dear mother. And for these nearly three weeks on my back, I have thought of you all more than a hundred times. What a nice thing is a good home. Don't think I am homesick, mother, you know I can say all these things and still not be homesick. When a fellow is sick and all broke up he can't help saying soft things. But I know if you had been here or I had been there I should not be where I am. Some of the fellows here are awful rough in their talk. They wasn't very sick and they are joking me and a young fellow in Co. E. because we are talking so much about our home and our mothers. I don't deny that I long to see my dear mother, and when the tears come into his eyes I know the poor boy that lays next to me is thinking of home too.

Don't think for a minute, mother, that I am dying. I am getting better and in a few days will rejoin my Co., which is now at Richmond, about 20 miles from here. It will seem like going home almost, to get back to my dear old Company. The nights are getting freezing cold and they tell me the lakes are covered with ice, and lately I dreamed of laying on my stomach and drinking cold icewater through the air holes. I suppose it's because I am always so dry.

They say that a few days ago three hundred soldiers came down from Ft. Abercrombie, 130 miles from here. They left everything quiet; in fact the Indian war seems at an end unless the upper Sioux turn on us.

Colonel Sibley[2] has recovered all the white prisoners and nearly 2,000 Indian prisoners. The question seems to be whether to let the Sioux remain or drive them from the homes of their ancestors into some western reservation. It seems likely that they will be driven away. Mother, this whole Indian question is wrong. Lying on my sick bed here, I can't help thinking of the wrongdoing of the government toward the Indians. I am losing heart in this war against the Indians. When you come to think that all this beautiful country along the Minnesota River was bought for 2 cents an acre and that the government still owes them this pitiful sum for it, I am sorry for them. The boys tell me I am no better than an Indian when I talk about it, but I can't help it. God made this country and gave it to the Indians. After a while along comes Columbus with his three cockleshell boats, takes possession of all the continent in the name of the Almighty, Queen Isabella of Spain, and the Indians are treated as wild beasts. I often think as I have heard father say, "if this is the spirit of the present Christianity, God will damn it."

I don't expect we will have a brush with the Indians unless we go farther west. The boys at Richmond are having good times, hunting deer and bear and catching fish. The lakes are clear and cool and full of fish.

---

2. Henry Hastings Sibley was born in Detroit in 1811 and spent practically his whole life on the frontier. He early engaged in the fur trade and in 1835 located at Mendota, at the mouth of the Minnesota River, where he built the first house in modern Minnesota. Here he lived until 1862, when he removed to St. Paul. Mr. Sibley was largely instrumental in securing the erection of Minnesota Territory and he served as its delegate in Congress from 1849 to 1853. He was elected first governor of the state, serving from 1858 to 1860; in 1862 he was commissioned by Governor Ramsey to take charge of the state troops in the Sioux War. By his wise and energetic course he succeeded in largely suppressing the outbreak and rescuing the captive whites when the federal government in response to urgent appeals by the state authorities sent General Pope to take charge of the situation. [*Wisconsin Magazine of History*]

We don't know where we are to winter, likely as not just where we are. My dear mother I am out of money. I haven't got the three dollars yet I wrote for the last time. I got to borrow a stamp to send this letter, but its alright. Mother, how does the new house come on? Have you got in it yet? Have you dug the potatoes yet? Does brother W. kill many prairie chickens this fall, or hasn't he got any ammunition? Has father got the stable plastered up warm? The blue clay in the bottom of the creek is all right for that.

Mother, don't you hate to leave the dear old cabin this winter for the new house? I love to think of that best of beds under those long, oak shingles, warped and twisted, that let in the rain and snow in my face. I would give all this world if I owned it, if I could sleep there tonight. Did the corn get ripe? Has father broke the colts? Has brother W. broke the steers so they can haul things? How is Father Cartwright? Has father killed any game this fall, what is it? Mother, as to the money I sent home, I want you or father to use it for anything you want. All I want is the first payment on that land so that is clear I don't care for the rest. You must get some apple trees if you have not already, and get a stand of bees. You ought to raise your own honey. I would like very much to hear from you mother. I haven't heard from home since I left La Crosse, I do not complain. There may be letters somewhere for me. Remember mother, a letter in your own handwriting. Love to all, to yourself, father, brothers and sister.

Your soldier boy.
Chauncey

NEW RICHMOND, MINN.,
HD. QUARTERS CO., G. 25TH REGT.
WIS., VOL. INFT., OCTOBER 28TH.

Dear Folks at Home:

Since my last you see I have made a change. I am now with the company at New Richmond. Andy Adams of Mondovi and one of the Mann brothers and myself came up in one of the Wells Fargo stages. The captain ordered us to the hotel as he tho't we was not strong enough for camp yet. I got your last letter the day before we left St. Cloud and what you told me about exposing myself after having the measles scared me just a bit. I had been walking about for three days and when I crossed the streets the wind was cold and so strong it would nearly throw me down and I had nothing but my summer drawers. Our women nurses didn't warn us a bit, but told me I should go out and get strength. I was glad enough to get out doors once more. I think I am getting all right. I was pretty sick the doctor told me, just as if I didn't know my own feelings. The Ladies' Aid Society was real kind. One old lady who did not belong to the society would come nearly every day with some sour candy and give it to all of us because our mouths tasted bad of the fever. She said she had a dear boy somewhere in the South and she hoped someone would be good to her boy if he got sick.

I tell you it seemed awful good to see the faces of my old chums. I had been away from them nearly four weeks and it seemed that many months.

They are busy building log houses to winter in. They are building 18 houses for store buildings and quarters. It is getting cold and the weather makes them hustle. The boys are still in tents tho it is freezing every night. The rest of the left wing have gone up to Paynesville to winter, four companies. I woke up this morning with a pain in my stomach. I told Elder Harwood of it and he told me not to eat any more biscuit before going to bed. We have a nice hotel and lots to eat and I am hungry all the time. They give us wild rice, bo't of the Indians, twice a day, and it is good. The Landlord said it was nearly gone and the Indians were gone and he didn't know when he could get any more. I like to hear him talk about the Indians. He said they had been cheated and lied to by the government contractors, and that bro't on all the trouble. He said he lived amongst them all his life and they were good people unless they were drunk.

I have lost fifteen and a half pounds in weight the three weeks past. I forgot to tell you I found a letter from you dated the 10th here in the Captain's hands. He forgot to send it to me. I am glad father has such good luck killing deer and bear this fall. Thank goodness old dog Prince was close by when the bear made that rush for father. He no doubt saved father's life. I hope the poor dog's jaw is not broken. The bear's jaw of course was too strong for him. Don't skim the milk for dear old Prince, give it to him with the cream on it until he can eat meat. We have bear and deer close to this place but you will believe me, I would dearly like to be with father in his hunts, long enough at least to help him kill two or three fat bears.

Don't fear but I will be careful dear mother of my health, you scared me when you explained about cousin Ben's death a month after he got up from the measles. I have had the measles, and "theys done gone" as Topsey said, in *Uncle Tom's Cabin.*

Rumors of Indians coming back on the war path is the talk among the boys in the hotel tonight. The sky is all lighted up some ten miles away by prairie fires tonight. The boys say it means Indians. My room is about 8 by 10 feet and the light from the prairie fire makes a shadow on the wall. Some of the boys talk like they wanted dreadfully to get into a scrimmage with the Sioux. It must be I aint a good soldier, I dont think it is fear, but I am all the time thinking of One Eye and his son and wife that came to our house so many times to get flour and coffee, and the times I played with their boys and sat on their buffalo robes and ate elk steak and venison steak by their wigwam fires. You know we wondered that they never came back any more, and father said they were afraid of their lives because the Dacotas and Minnesota Sioux had declared war and to save their lives they had gone west.

I don't deny that I sometimes think of Owena, the Chief's daughter that father plagued me about, and wonder where she is.

Bishop Whipple[3] says the government has never kept its word of payment for the land and the rations promised the Indians. That man Whipple must be another William Penn. He has always been the Indian's friend in Minnesota. I read in the *Sentinel* yesterday that he had visited the White House in Washington and plead with President Lincoln with tears in his eyes that the government should pay these Sioux their promised annuity and that would stop the war. Why don't they do it? I am a white man's son and I like my own people but I can never forget what Chief One Eye told me in his wigwam on the Three Mile Creek that the white chief at Washington was a liar because they never got their annuity and their beef was tough and unfit to eat.

I hope father will not sell my 40 even at a hundred dollars profit. I like Wisconsin best of all yet.

They are all in bed but me, so good night.

Your boy,
Chauncey.

---

3. Henry Benjamin Whipple was born and educated in New York; in 1859 he was consecrated first bishop of the Episcopal Church in Minnesota. He acquired great influence among the Sioux and Ojibway and by them was given a name meaning "Straight Tongue." In the face of much popular opposition he maintained a friendly stand toward the Sioux at the time of the troubles of 1862 and emphasized the responsibility of the whites for the trouble through official neglect and misdoing on the part of individuals. [*Wisconsin Magazine of History*]

NEW RICHMOND, MINN.
CO. G. 25TH REGT.
NOV. 4TH, 1862.

Dear sister Doe:

Your favor of Oct. 25th rec'd yesterday. It seemed so good to me that I read it over twice before stopping. I am just like other soldiers I suppose, crazy to get letters from dear ones at home. I wrote mother only a day or two ago but that makes no difference, I am glad for an excuse to write home. I told mother that I did not expect to leave St. Cloud for some days but we left the next day in one of those big Wells Fargo coaches you told me so much about. We had four horses on the coach and they trotted nearly all the way, 20 miles, to this place. I found the boys fat as pigs except them that were sick with measles. Some ten or a dozen were sick.

You said you received $10 in one of my letters. I sent $30 altogether in the two letters. I also sent my clothes. Did you get them?

It is now quite certain we will winter here as they have commenced building cabins. It is about 225 miles from home, just a nice sleigh ride.

I could get home for about $7 but that would buy a good many things you need this coming winter, and maybe I could not get away. Be good enough to send me the *Tribune* or the Milwaukee *Sentinel*. We don't have anything here to read but Dutch papers. I want to get some papers or books this winter and maybe you better send me a few dollars. I was too good when I sent the last money to father and I shall be short before my next pay day which is in December. I am real glad you are making such headway in your books. You are father's girl alright. Do you know, sister, I used to think father was a curious kind of person because he differed with so many people, and I didn't know what to think about it, but I know now our father is a sensible man. He opened my eyes about this Indian question which I am finding every day to be true, and I believe his opinion about the slaveholders to be just as true. I cannot forget his words in the grove at Rufus Fuller's when we started for Alma after that big dinner. He said, "Be true to your country my boy, and be true to the flag, but before your country or the flag be true to the slave." I never saw tears in father's eyes before.

I am still in the tavern. I bought some packs the other day and paid $3 for them, a big price but I had to have them. Tell father to pick up a chopper if he can find one and set him to work at my expense in the big timber over northeast. We need a lot more rails. We need to keep dark about timber until we get some logs out of it. Cut the logs and mark them together and I will split them myself if I ever get back. Nobody knows of the timber but Mr. Amidon and nobody will ever touch it. Mr. Amidon got a dozen or so logs there last winter for the mill. I counted the stumps last spring when I speared those beaver there last spring.

Poor old dog Prince and I had a lot of fun on that creek. How is Prince getting on from that fight with that bear? I wish father would be more careful in shooting at bears. Prince may not always be near by to lock jaws with the black devils. I often think of the night I slept with Prince in my arms in Traverse Valley. The fire had gone out and it was dark as tar. When a fox would bark he would tremble and raise his head and growl. When that deer snorted in the brush and run he nearly scared me to death as he jumped out from the blanket and run after him. Give the old dog a hug for me. There is lots of game here and I wish I had old Prince with me.

Obed Hilliard and I have bought a lot of traps and as soon as I get strong I am going to set them. The boys have shot a lot of rats and minks with their muskets.

The news came just now that McClellan had captured 30,000 rebs and had cornered the rest of Lee's army, and the war was at an end. We hear things like this nearly every day. Nobody believes it.

Your brother,
Chauncey.

FT. WILDCAT, RICHMOND, MINN.
NOV. 10TH, 1862.

Dear Mother:

I believe my last was written to Doe, anyway I will write this time to you. I like letters from father and Sister Doe, too, awful well, but if you could hear what I hear every day about things and persons at home, you would hear the fathers talked about and you would hear that the sisters and brothers were nice people, but the mothers in the daily talk of the soldiers are the best persons in the world. Well now this may sound like I am homesick but I ain't. I was going to say, we are to have inspection of arms in a little while and I tho't I would put in the time until then writing. The snow fell to the depth of 5 inches last night and the woods this forenoon was full of soldiers hunting deer. A bear was seen by one of the boys but nothing but some partridges and rabbits was killed. Until day before yesterday the lakes were full of ducks and geese. I never saw so many ducks. The boys have killed lots of them. I purchased a pair of moccasins, paid $3.50 for them, a big price but had to have them. I want to do some shooting pretty soon. The orderly has informed us that there will be no inspection of arms. I noticed in the *Sentinel* that Gilmanton was exempt from draft. That is all the Gilmanton folks wanted, so they said. Now we will see how much those moneyed ones will give now that they are in no danger of draft. I was out on drill day before yesterday, the first time in six weeks.

The cabins are nearly done and I shall be glad to get out of the hotel with the boys although I like things here. The commissary building is full of beef, pork, and flour and good things to eat. The company will be divided into squads with a cook for each squad. Obed Hilliard is the cook for our squad, Obe and I are in partnership in trapping. The lakes and the Sioux River that runs by our camp are full of mink and rats. I found a big black mink in a trap of one of the other boys last night just below camp. His hide was worth $8. I was half tempted to take him out. The boys are playing just these tricks every day on each other. I nearly forgot to tell you I had bowel trouble the other day and Sergeant McKay gave me a dose of burnt whiskey. It was the first whiskey I ever drank. It helped my bowel trouble and I suppose from what the boys tell me it made me do some strange things. Men Bump and Chet Ide of Mondovi have been laughing at me and telling me that I was a shame to old topers that I talked stuff and got out Bill Hill's drum and pounded it. Anyway I am alright now. I have no more news to write this time. Mr. Ball sends his respects to Mr. Cartwright, and Mr. McKay sends his regards to father.

I was just closing this letter when one of the boys came into my room and told me the Indians were burning Paynesville, where the other four companies of the left wing are posted. I went to the window and sure enough there was a big light on the sky in the direction of Paynesville. I have been waiting a half hour for later news. If it meant Indians I knew we would be notified by courier. As we have heard nothing it means just a prairie fire, so good night mother.

Your loving boy,
Chauncey.

RICHMOND, MINN.,
NOV. 20, 1862.

Dear Parents:—

I had no letters the past week but look for one this afternoon. Things go on rather quiet most of the time. Our log shanties are all finished and I am now with the boys. I'll tell you, I am keeping a diary and I will give you a copy of it for a week in this letter:—

Nov. 10—Took a shave today. One of the boys said my beard made me look like a goat. Had my first dinner at the shanty, Obe is a good cook. Supply train loaded with provisions went by for Sauk Center and Paynesville. Some men, trappers I guess, from the Red River country went toward St. Cloud, they stopped for dinner. Said all was quiet in the up country. They wore leggins like Indians and their stories if true, made them out more savage. According to their talk all Indians are red devils.

Nov. 11—A nice Indian summer day, a smoky, hazy, dreamy day. Took my gun and went rat hunting. Shot five but got only four. Came back to camp hungry as a dog. Had a glorious supper of beef, bread, potatoes, cranberry sauce, and pie.

A big supply train bound for Fort Abercrombie pulled in for the night. Gen. Pope has ordered all infantry south. We may get to see Dixie yet. Hurrah! Snow all gone and big prairie fires to the east tonight.

Nov. 12—No letter from home today, plague on it. Wrote one to George Wooster. Beautiful weather. Men Bump just from St. Cloud reports another one of the boys dead from measles. I believe I am all right except my wind ain't quite so good on a long double quick. Nothing to do, went out and shot a rat. Some of the lakes are covered with rat houses thick as hay cocks and as big. Sold my hides for 10 cents a piece. Boys trying their guns at a mark, found a great deal of fault with them. I found some papers at the hotel called *The Dacota Friend,* that I have been reading. They were left by a woman who had been stopping. This paper was a missionary paper for the Indians and had letters in it from Bishop Whipple. He is certainly a good man. I read some of his letters about the honesty of the Indians when the white man was honest with them. It made me think of good old One Eye and his band that came so many times to our place. I spoke of Bishop Whipple to the trappers and what he said of their honesty, but they said Whipple was an old woman in breeches.

Nov. 13—I dreamed last night of One Eye's band, of the boys that

I played with, and when we got hungry how we went to Chief Charley's tepee and found his mother cleaning the entrails of a beaver which she intended for soup. The boy talked to her in Sioux and she unfolded some buckskins and a robe or two and gave us a big hunk of elk steak. We put it on the fire and she went back to her job of dressing the beaver guts. In my dreams I saw the beautiful buffalo robes we lay upon while our steak was roasting. I could even smell them just as they smelt four years ago.

In this miserable Indian war I often wonder what has become of Lightfoot (father gave him that name because he could beat me in a race) and of his brothers and of Owena. They promised to come back in the fall of 1860 when they broke camp the spring before two miles below us but they never came. I haven't lived long, but long enough to think this is a strange world. When I think of the Indians and remember how good they were to me and my father and mother, and reading in this *Dacota Friend* paper how the traders have made them drunk in order to cheat them, and how the government bought 35,000,000 acres of them and has been owing them for it against their promise for thirty years, and because they were starving and broke into a warehouse for food, and this brought on a war. I am for the Indians as much as the whites.

Nov. 14—Cold and freezing this morning. A cannon from Fort Abercrombie came by this morning. They fired it a few times just for fun. Obed Hilliard and I went hunting, shot five rats, one partridge, and one rabbit. On return to camp found a supply train in corral near us and 300 cavalry as guard. The fife and drum were out tonight, in honor of our guests I suppose. The visitors have some big fires going tonight and the crowds around them are very happy. The cavalry men who have been on the frontier are full of Indian yarns. I don't like their talk. If half they tell about their own rascally tricks is true, there is plenty of reason for the Indians to fight and fight to the death.

Nov. 15—There was quite a wild time last night. Some beer was stolen from the saloon and farmers came in this morning claiming soldiers stole their chickens. The cavalry did it. Our boys denied it and I am sure they told the truth. The cavalry made quite a show as they dashed off after the wagon train. I went to church today, the first time in a long while. Cold and freezing tonight. I nearly froze my fingers on dress parade.

Nov. 16—Everything froze tight this morning. This has been a lonesome day. Molasses was rationed out, the first since we came. It run awful slow. Drilled this afternoon. Snow began falling while we were drilling. The Colonel arrived from Paynesville. I have been reading all the evening in Bishop Whipple's paper, *The Dacota Friend*. I have made up my mind the Indians are not to blame for this war. It is the traders, the contractors, the trappers, and the Indian agents. O, the injustice of the strong against the weak in this world.

Nov. 17–18—Went hunting deer, no luck at all. I shall let the deer go to grass hereafter and hunt for rabbits only. Late this afternoon had a tilt snowballing. The boys had a lively time dodging my balls. They didn't know I had kept a pile of stones at every fence corner for years for blackbirds, and that a blackbird's head at ten steps was an easy mark. The ice on the Sioux is fine. Bought a pair of skates and had a little fun on them. There is a big farmer, a Swede, three miles up river with a nice family of boys and girls. If the ice is good, will go up there in the morning.

Nov. 19—Was on the river skating all the forenoon. Ice not quite safe on the rapids. Several of the boys on a drunk. Had quite a scrap but no one much hurt. Had a spelling school tonight. Word came late tonight that we were to go south in a week, hope it is true.

Your boy,
Chauncey.

Nov. 21—Went out to visit my traps and found several of them frozen in. Found four rats in the traps set in the houses. Most of the traps in the run ways except in springy places were frozen in. Caught a mink near the bridge over the Sioux in a little spring.

This afternoon skated three miles up the river to the house of a Swede who is one of the first settlers in this county. He has a big family of boys and rosy-cheeked girls.

I ate a late dinner with them. He was a great talker and told me a lot about the wild times he saw when he first struck the country. He was a friend to the Indians. They always camped near his house when trapping up and down the Sioux River, in the fall and spring.

This man told me the war began by a dog biting an Indian. The Indian shot the dog and the whites shot the Indian and a band of the Sisseton Sioux hearing of this and nearly starved for government rations that never came, broke into a government warehouse and from this the war started that has cost the nation, so the papers say, round 40 million of dollars. This man told me he never lost a cent by a sober Indian. He had a room in his house called the Indian room where he always put them in the winter when they called. They preferred to sleep in tepees in the fall and spring when they came to trap for furs and to gather wild rice. They were the Santee Sioux, the band that One Eye and Chief Charley belonged to. He showed me a buffalo trail on a steep hillside leading down to the river, which he said had been worn for a hundred years.

He said the Indians never killed a friend if they knew it. The whites were more revengeful, they shot at every Indian, good and bad. He told me a lot more I can't write down. When I left for camp tonight it was dark. I looked at a few of the traps I had set but found nothing.

I believe I am as much of an Indian, as the boys say, as white man and I can't deny it. I am awfully tired tonight.

Nov. 22—I heard this morning that Little Crow, Chief of the Sioux had committed suicide. If it is true it is because he has lost faith in the great "white Chief" at Washington and the broken promises of the government. There are some things in this war that make me feel that I am an infidel. Why does God crush all these poor Indians and give it all to the white because he has wealth. They owned this land from ocean to ocean by the best title on earth given by God himself and yet because we are stronger we drive them away from the homes of their fathers and the graves of their ancestors and claim that Christ is on our side.

I have been studying the *Dacota Friend* the woman left here in the hotel, and I believe there is something terribly wrong in this war. I know the Indians have been wronged and mistreated. But what can a fellow like me do? I could not eat any supper tonight and I dared not tell the boys what I was thinking about. I knew they would joke me and make fun of me. I feel that Obed Hilliard is nearer to me than any of the boys and yet he says the Indians ought to be shot. I seem to think different from any of them. I may not be right but I can't help it. I know I think as Bishop Whipple does that all the wrong in this war is on the side of the whites. I am sleepy and it is ten o'clock.

Nov. 23.—The landlord of the hotel gave me to understand this morning that I could not use any more of his writing paper, as I had left the house for the camp. Of course it's all right but it bothers me because I can't write where the boys are bothering. We had a drill this forenoon. The captain said we would get pay tomorrow and I am glad. I have two pages in my memoranda of debit and credit accounts to be settled.

Nov. 24—Marching orders to be in readiness to start for Fort

Snelling, I guess it's a go this time. The notice came last night and all my traps are set miles away on the river and lakes. Obie said when the moon comes up tonight if you will gather in the traps I'll do the other work.

It was after midnight when I got back with all the traps and my light is the only one burning as I write this last word.

Nov. 25—It was a lonely trip I made last night up the river and over the lakes picking up traps. I thought of so many things on that trip and I was not quite satisfied that Obe asked me to get the traps alone but I made the trip just the same. In the woods between the lakes where the moon shone in spots under the pine trees I thought I saw figures of Indians but I would brace up and walk right up to them and I always found them stumps or trees. I can't say I was really afraid, but I was miles away in an Indian country and sometimes my heart would pump a little hard.

Final orders to begin our return march to Fort Snelling near St. Paul came late last night. We were up bright and early. Some of the boys said they were fixing all night to get ready. I was hard to wake, because I had gone to bed so late after my night's jaunt gathering in my traps. I had paid a dollar and a quarter a piece for the traps, and the merchant said I had had such bad luck, he would take them back at cost and charge me $2 for the use of them. I thanked him from the bottom of my heart as I had expected a much harder deal. Some of the fellows, one or two from Mondovi had spent a good part of the night at one of the saloons just across the Sioux River and they were singing "Dixie" and "Johnny comes marching home" long before the morning drum beat. I was scared for a moment thinking that the march had commenced when I heard them singing, but hearing my chum snoring at my side, I went to sleep again.

All the forenoon its been Dixie, Dixie. A lot of the nearby settlers came in to see the boys go away. Some of them said its all right for us to go south, they weren't afraid any more the Indians had been scared away, others wished we would stay. I think there were four or five pretty girls from the Sioux River that felt sorry for reasons of their own to see the boys go away. It was near noon when we started out in hit or miss order for St. Cloud. We straggled into St. Cloud late in the evening. Every fellow looked out for his own sleeping quarters. It was cold. The Captain said, "Get the best quarters you can." I slept under the flap of a tent between barrels rolled up in two blankets with a freezing west wind like so much cold water pouring over my face all night. I was awakened in the morning by that song so dear to the south, Dixie. I would think more of what the song means, if the fellows had their heads.

We have been late this morning, November twenty-sixth, in starting. I have put in the time writing my notes.

Nov. 26—I am tired tonight; marched all day with heavy overcoat, haversack, gun, and two big blankets. I made but 18 miles and when it began to get dark I dropped out of the squad I was with and went to a private house where I saw a light shining among the trees. A young woman and child were the only persons there. She told me her husband had gone to the war and she was carrying on the farm alone with a little help her brother gave her who came once in a while. She told me she had but one bed in the house but I was welcome if I could sleep on the lounge in the kitchen. I asked to sleep on the floor, but she said, "No." I told her where I slept the night before and she just looked at me without saying a word. She asked me why my mother let me go into the army when I was so young. When I told her I tried to get my mother's consent a year before, she said, "O, you must be a crazy fellow."

Nov. 27—I was up and on the road this morning by daylight. I was anxious to catch up with the boys I knew were ahead of me. To tell the whole truth, I shed a few tears because I could not keep up with the crowd. Obed had told me and Sergeant McKay that I was not over the effects of the measles and that I should take it easy. Father wrote me too, before leaving the hotel at Richmond, "Be patient and not try to do too much, you will need to save your strength for months." Just the same I am mad that the boys are going to beat me to St. Paul.

Nov. 28th—Fort Snelling, Minn. Arrived this noon. A few of the company still here, most of them come and gone. The right wing of our Reg't came down the Minnesota some days ago bringing with them 1,700 captured Sioux, wives, children, and old men and women of the hostiles. They are camped on the bottoms just below the Fort at the junction of the Minnesota and Mississippi rivers. They are a broken-hearted, ragged, dejected looking lot. They have a million dogs almost, and you can hear them barking for miles. There are 156 tepees. A Minnesota Reg't is in charge of them and no soldier is allowed inside the tepees. Papooses are running about in the snow barefoot and the old Indians wear thin buckskin moccasins and no stockings. Their ponies are poor and their dogs are starved. They are going to be shipped West into the Black Hills country. Like the children of Israel in the Bible story they are forced to go forever from the homes of their childhood and the graves of their fathers to dwell in the mountains and on the barren plains of a strange land. I lifted up the flaps of a number of their tepees and looked in. Every time I looked in I met the gaze of angry eyes. Nearly all of them were alike. Mothers with babies at their breasts, grandmothers and grandsires sat about smouldering fires in the center of the tepee, smoking their long stemmed pipes, and muttering their plaints in the soft guttural tones of the Sioux. The white man's face was their hate and their horror and they showed it by hate in their eyes and their black lowering brows. Why shouldn't they? What had they done? What was their crime? The white man had driven them from one reservation to another. They were weary and broken hearted and desperate at the broken promises of the government. And when they took up arms in desperation for their homes and the graves of their sires they are called savages and red devils. When we white people do the same things we are written down in history as heroes and patriots. Why this difference? I can't see into it. I often think of what father said of justice in the world. That is, that it is the winning party the lions of the earth, that write its history. He said, "Cataline, had anybody but his bitter enemies written his history, might have been shown to be a good man." I have been fooling around the Indian camps all day and my company are all gone home. From where I sit writing these notes in a little niche on the side of the Fort overlooking the camp below I can see the sentinels pacing their rounds and hear the yelping of hungry Indian dogs. My fingers are numb. The cold west wind hits me here and I must quit. I must look for a warm place to sleep tonight and start for home in the morning by the way of Hudson and Eau Claire.

LIFE AT OLD CAMP RANDALL

CAMP RANDALL, MADISON, WIS.
CO. G. 25TH WIS. VOL. INFT.
DEC. 16, 1862

Dear Parents:

After just one week of varying incident from the time of leaving my old dear home I am seated to write to you. We did not find our regiment at Winona as we expected, they had gone to La Crosse. There were 27 of us in the crowd so we hired three liveries and drove all night and reached La Crosse at 6 o'clock in the morning. We nearly swamped in the Black river crossing McGilvery's ferry the ice was running so, but we got over all right. We stayed in La Crosse one night and came on to Madison the next night. The people of La Crosse were good to us, they gave us a fine dinner in the biggest hall in town but mother it did not taste half as good as the last one you gave me of bear meat and venison and hot biscuit and honey. It may be I did not do right when I sneaked out of the house and got Billy and rode away without saying good bye, but I couldn't help it. I knew it hurt you to say good-bye and that's why I did it.

Well, we are in Madison, the Capital of the state. How long we are to stay nobody knows. They say we need drilling and must get more disciplined before we go to the front. Well I hope we won't stay here long. These barracks are awful cold, and my bunk is on the top tier, next to the shingles—too hot in the evening—cold in the morning. I am wearing father's moccasins yet. I didn't get time to buy me boots in La Crosse or Winona.

Tell father to use my money and buy him some more. We are to be paid soon and I will send you some money. You need not lay it up as you did before but use it, and don't think of me, I am all right. I never want to see father wear patches again. I don't believe this war is for long. I expect to be home next year to help with the work. Maybe not, but we'll see.

I forgot to tell you that we came in the cars to Madison from La Crosse. It was a new experience to me, I was wide awake the whole way. I was afraid we were off the track every time we crossed a switch or came to a river. At the towns, girls swarmed on the platforms to ask the boys for their pictures and to kiss the best looking ones. A young Frenchman, we called him the pony of the regiment because he was so small and quick, got the most kisses. He was so short the boys held him by the legs so he could reach down out the windows to kiss the girls. Many times some old fellow held the girls up so she could be reached. It was fun anyway.

I never think but I am all right, except when I try to double quick for a half hour or so. My wind gives out. Lieutenant Parr says, "Your measles stay with you yet." "Warm weather," he says, "will fix you all right." Love to all.

Your son,
Chauncey.

MADISON, WIS., DEC. 25TH, 1862,
CO. G., 25TH REGT.

Dear Mother:

You see my paper don't have the regulation picture on it of Soldiers in file or in battle array. I am tired of such flummery. The meaning of the whole thing is to make money for the inventor and not for the soldier. We are told that the life of the Nation is at stake, and every fellow that enlists offers himself as a martyr to save his country. I was thinking these things over last, about 2 P.M. in the morning when I was nearly froze and the relief guard came round and I was off duty to go to my tent and get some sleep. It seems like foolery to the common soldier that for two hours we must stand in a temperature of 30 or 40 degrees when we are a thousand miles from the enemy. I had to walk and walk to keep from freezing. The mercury was down near 40 below zero and the guard house where we sat down between reliefs or lay down was little better than out doors. The health of our Regiment is none too good. One man dies on an average every day. As I write this letter the drum is beating. The food we get is to blame for our bad health. The boys threaten a riot every day for the bad beef and spoilt bread issued to us and all this in our home state of Wisconsin. I went to meeting yesterday both morning and evening. In the morning at the Baptist, in the evening at the Episcopal church. The preacher discussed the state of the Union. I thot he talked a bit like a traitor. He was sorry the states should go to war over the question of slavery. He hoped the Union would be preserved and he thot *Uncle Tom's Cabin* was much to blame for the war. Capt. Dorwin said the preacher ought to live in South Carolina. There is talk that we will get pay tomorrow. I have sent a record of our company home. Hope you got it. I shall send you a lot of clothing just before we leave. Remember me to Uncle Edward Cartwright. It was kind of him to ask so often about me. I wonder where Ez and Ed are. They don't say a word. You remember they went in the 2nd Cavalry.

I am glad father had such good luck getting deer this fall, you will have lots of venison this winter. It is too bad the Elk are all gone or killed off. I know father is sorry. He blamed the Sioux Indians for scaring his game but the St. Louis hunters and the Farringtons of Mondovi have spoiled his hunting more than the Indians. I hope he will stop hunting bears alone. Its a dangerous business. Old Prince is a dear good dog but a bear is too much for him at close quarters. Is his jaw all right again? Every letter I get from home I expect to hear of Jenny's death. She is bound to rub her red blanket off in the brush and the first hunter that sees her will shoot her for a wild deer. I wonder what Claffin's people tho't when she ran in their bedroom and laid down to get away from the dogs.

Poor thing eight miles from home with no friend near, raced by dogs until her tongue hung out, and to save her life rushed into the open door of the Claffin home. Poor Jenny Deer. With four bullet marks on her legs and body and one thru her red blanket and the damned dogs racing her for life. Poor thing. Poor thing. I can't help it, but these things make me homesick.

I'm ashamed of myself, Dear Mother, Good Bye.

From your son
Chauncey.

MADISON, WISCONSIN, JAN. 6TH, 1863.
HD. QUARTERS 25TH REGT., WIS.

Dear Sister:

I am sure you would smile if you could get a view of Co. G. as I can see them from where I sit. You would say, "What a writing school." I can count more than 40 of the boys writing letters to their mothers or their girls. Mostly to their girls. Its easy to tell, if a fellow is writing to his mother he don't squirm and cover his paper when some guy looks over his shoulder. There is a lot of such teasing. The only way is to get away up in the top bunks out of reach and hold their portfolios on their laps for a desk. I came off guard this morning after the coldest night of the winter. My beat was long side the railroad track on a high bank where the wind cut me from all sides. I set my gun down and run back and forth to keep from freezing my toes. The snow sifted in the path and kept it soft and mealy. The Legislature had some extra work at the capitol last night. I could see the light at the top of the dome until after midnight.

No pay yet though they keep promising it. Went to the Episcopal church last Sunday. Say, don't they put on style though? I compared them in my mind to our little bunch in that two by four schoolhouse in Gilmanton. The preacher came out in a black dress and talked about things I couldn't understand, but the music was nice when I came away. If I was any better in heart, it was because of the music and not for anything the preacher said. A lot of the boys celebrated Christmas and New Year to their sorrow. Some of them were put in jail up town and two of them are there yet. Nearly every other house between here and the Capitol sells beer and by the time the lovers of grog get into town they are full to running over with "When Johnny comes marching home." There was close to a mutiny of the two regiments here the other day because so many of the boys had been arrested and jailed in the city. The 30th. regiment and several companies of the 25th came out without officers, formed in ranks swearing they would go up and storm the city of Madison, if necessary, and release their comrades in jail. Feeling ran so high that I took my place in the ranks without much heart in it to tell the truth. I was glad when our officers came around and explained that we were mutineers and in violation of the rules of war and that we should disband.

I had no pity in my heart for the fellows in jail and I was glad for an excuse to sneak back to headquarters. We have some good fellows in our company who are devils when they are in drink. And we have about four who are devils drunk or sober. While I am writing these, the boys are singing Dixie in a great chorus. This awful weather makes us hanker for the warmer south and, since there is no hope of home. All seems quiet on the Potomac.

I see by the papers that the churches are urged to pray for the end of the war. They have had several spells at this and the battles have been harder and the slaughter greater. The churches south have been doing the same thing. It would seem that God ought to pity the slave and help our side, but will he? I know what father would say. He would quote Napoleon, who said, "Put your trust in well drilled troops and keep your powder dry." I remember the last time I heard him say this, when Elder Morse was visiting us and they were talking about the wickedness of slavery about which they both agreed. Father disputed the Elder's opinion that God presided over the movements and affairs of earth. He cited slavery and the wicked wars of the earth and the crimes of the liquor traffic as being inconsistent with the character of a just God. Elder Morse agreed with father this far, that they were not in harmony with the Divine plan, but were tolerated for some reason not given to man to know.

Have father tell Elder Morse, I thank him for his kind words. His son Henry is about and able to eat his rations every day. I hope you wont sell your land as you talk of doing. I got a letter from G——— the other day and answered it. He thinks McClellan is a traitor. Lots of us think the same. Our Captain is a wise man and he says McClellan has been waiting and waiting when he should have been marching and fighting. I am awful sorry that Freemont was set down on by Lincoln. I am with Freemont as many of the boys are. I have no heart in this war if the slaves cannot go free. Freemont wanted to set them free as fast as we came to them. I am disappointed in Lincoln. I remember a talk father had with Uncle Ed. Cartwright, who was blaming the war on the Abolitionists. It made father mad and he talked back pretty hot. He said I have a boy who wants to go to the war and I would give his life as cheerfully as Abraham offered his son if necessary that the slaves might be freed. Father meant all right though it seemed hard, but I love him all the more for it, although I suppose I am the boy he meant for the sacrifice. We are all anxious to go south, though none of us that I know are anxious to get shot for any cause. Direct as before to Camp Randall. Love to all, mother, father and brothers.

Your brother,
Chauncey.

CAMP RANDALL, MADISON, WIS.
HD. QUARTERS 25 REGT. WIS. VOL. INFTY.

Dear Mother:

This is a fine morning and the 29th. of January, 1863. How the time flies. Your last letter came day before yesterday. I am awfully glad father had such good luck killing deer. You will have plenty of good meat for the winter. You wish I could have a taste along with you. You bet I do too, but it can't be, so we must not think of it. We came close to a row with the 30th regiment yesterday. The Colonel in command of a squad came down to put some of our boys in the guard house. The word spread like wild fire and a rush was made for the barracks where the boys were taken, and it took but a minute to get them from the 30th men and the 30th Colonel was glad to get back to his regiment. The boys are threatening revolt against the commissary. Our meat and bread is a fright and a big share of the men in both regiments are ripe for mischief. I get a lunch nearly every day at a little grocery just outside the fence. I get a glass of cider, a handful of crackers and a nice piece of Swiss cheese for ten cents. They are Swiss Germans that run the grocery and the girl that clerks has the blackest hair and eyes I ever saw. She has been in this country three years and talks very good English. She has a brother in the Swiss army and when she brags the Swiss soldiers and how much nicer they are than we Yankees, she shows the prettiest white teeth as she smiles.

There is a rumor that we are to be paid soon, anyway before we go South. Rumor is such a liar we don't know what to believe. It is quite sure we will be assigned to the Southwest somewhere. Perhaps to Vicksburg, where the rebs are making a grand stand, perhaps to post duty on some of the river points. Some of the boys pretend they would like to smell gun powder on the battle line before the war ends. I suppose they feel that way. I am learning some things. I find that men who talk the most are not always the bravest.

The news from Washington is bad. McClellan with his big army has gone into winter quarters instead of making an aggressive campaign toward Richmond. Gen. McClernand is doing far more good work than all the rest. Some of the boys are dreaming of home and a good time pretty soon, but the Richmond papers talk like the south was just beginning to wake up. Lots of poor fellows will bite the dust before the end yet.

Friday Jan. 30th. I took a run this morning up to the Adjutant's office and back, to try my wind. It is quite a distance from our barrack. I believe I am getting my legs and wind back, and I am awfully glad. Some of the poor fellows who were sick with me in St. Cloud, Minn., with measles, are losing ground. Orlando Adams of Mondovi says he has no wind any more. Nathan Mann says he has no vim any more and can't stand the drill exercises.

Lots of the boys are blue as whetstones. They say if they were only out of it, the Union might go to blazes. If they would take us where the traitors are, and give us a chance to fight, we would feel that we were doing something. But this dreadful sameness is wearing.

February 2nd. Dear Mother: Your latest letter came this morning. I hope you wont delay writing because news is scarce. Anything from home is news if it is in your hand writing and only about the dog or cat. No, I don't suppose we get the war news earlier than you do. I thank you for sending the paper of tea, altho you remember I don't love it especially. But I am sure this will be good coming from the best of mothers. I will drink it in memory of you and home. I have read somewhere that mothers were the best beings in the world and now I know it to be true. I trust I may live to come home and prove it to you. You think our officers should see that our bread and meat is good. My dear mother they dont have a word to say about it. It's in the hands of the contractors. Dont worry, we will live thru it, and if southern bullets don't get us, we will tell you all about it when we come home. So Henry Amidon is married. Well, well, Henry is a good boy and I hope he has made no mistake in his choice. So the world goes. I used to think Mrs. Amidon's doughnuts and milk gravy was better than ours. You don't care mother do you if I say this. She was a nice cook and after walking down to Beef river, and taking a swim with Henry, and by the time we got back to his home for a late dinner, things tasted mighty good.

I was just a bit of a fool two years ago next March when I tried to wade across the foot bridge up to my chin in ice water near the mill dam to visit Henry when his folks were in Vermont. I had to back out and when I got back to shore I was so numb that I ran clear down to Uncle Dan Loomis' place and back to start my blood circulating. I was so cold I couldn't put all my clothes on and ran half naked.

I guess I've strung this letter plenty long, and part of it I can't read myself. I expect to catch it from father about my spelling as usual, well thats alright, I ought to improve as I have bo't me a pocket dictionary. It looks so much like a testament that our Chaplain came along the other day and asked me what chapter I was reading. Well, he said, the testament is the only book that is better anyway. He is a good man and wants every soldier to have a testament.

Direct as before to Co. G. Camp Randall, Madison.

Your son, Chauncey.

Yours of recent date just received. I am glad you are knocking the split rail endways. Now we will have a good fence and no mistake.

We must not put any hollow logs in for a foundation like the one you told of in Ohio, where one end came on the outside and the other on the inside of the field. I never think of that story of the old sow trying to get into the field after the farmer had turned both ends on the outside, without a good laugh. It seems you have heard that small pox is prevalent here. Don't be scared. There was but three or four cases and they were in the 30th Regt. Deaths are frequent enough but from other causes. We are losing a man a day on an average. The boys are buried on a hill just above the camp, and the roll of the muffled drum and the blank discharge of a dozen muskets is the solemn reminder that another soldier has gone to his last bivouac. Father, I begin to hate war and I have seen nothing of it either. There is so much contention among the boys so much that we hear from the Potomac, about treachery, of McClellan and a never ending dispute about the freedom of the slaves. Just now too we are having a fearful rumpus about the rations. The boys are on the point of revolting against the government, the contractors or the state for the sour bread and stinking meat rationed out to us. The sickness of our Regt. is laid to bad food. Stuff they call coffee is made of various seeds.

It seems an outrage to get such treatment in the Capital of our State. Curse upon curse is heaped upon the contractors. We have appealed to the members of the Legislature but they can't help us. After we had drawn our rations of sour bread the other day some three hundred of the boys marched down and stormed the commissary with the sour loaves as ammunition. The next day we got better bread but it did not last long. We hear that it is made out of musty crackers and soap. I don't know I'm sure. I got a letter just this minute and dear, I am so glad. I can see you all gathered about the kitchen stove. Mother has just filled the tea kettle for morning, and father is filling the oven with kindling too wet for starting the fire in the morning and I can see myself cuddled up under the blankets just as mother used to leave me after saying good night under the open shakes with the snow drifting in upon me. I don't believe I am homesick, but if I could not recall in memory these pleasant days of my boyhood I am not quite sure but I should be. Tell mother I am just childish enough to recall that little trundle bed prayer and to repeat it in a whisper every night. I do it because it brings me closer to her but how I cannot tell.

We are going south pretty soon, we hear it rumored every day.

I got a letter yesterday from Fred Rosman. He recalled the times we hoed corn together in 1857. Fred and I layed great plans about killing chickens and sending them to Fountain City and selling to the steam boats.

What funny folks boys are anyway. We talked about a lot of things. Most of our schemes have come to naught. O the pity, that the world don't pan out as they expected. Dora said in her last letter that you were not so well. Your letter makes no mention of illness. I hope you are all right.

Your son,
Chauncey.

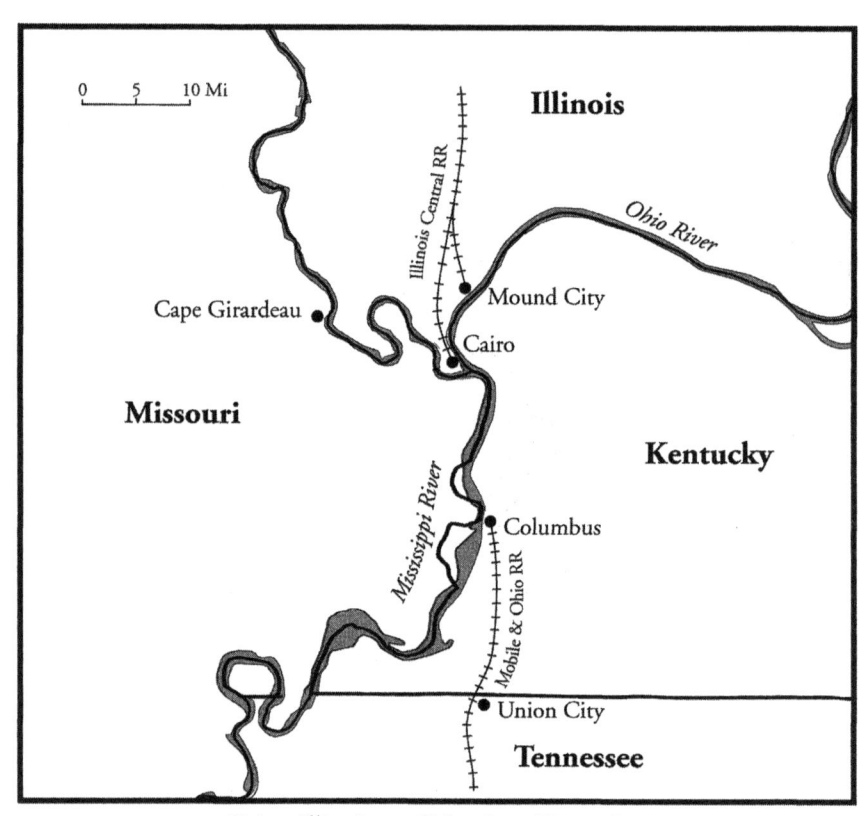

Cairo, Illinois, to Columbus, Kentucky.
February 19, 1863–May 31, 1863.

INTO THE SOUTHLAND

Columbus, Kentucky,
25th Regt. Wis. Volunteers.
February 28th, 1863.

Dear Sister:

Your letter came in due time. It was handed me yesterday by the orderly as I came off guard. You rate me pretty low on composition and spelling but I mean to do better. Yes, I sent my clothes the day before we left Madison. I directed the box in care of Giles Cripps at Trempealeau. Father will have to get it from there. It weighs about 100 pounds. You will know my knapsack by my name stamped on one of the shoulder straps. Barney Bull has a coat in my bundle, all the rest belongs to the Mondovi boys outside of my knapsack. Father should leave their clothes at Yankee Town,[1] where their folks will get them. I hope father won't wear my coat. I hate to see a civilian in soldier's dress. If I ever get back it will do me for some time, and if I don't get back give it to some poor soldier in the neighborhood. You did not say anything of my letter written on the eve of leaving Madison for Cairo, Illinois. Of course you have it by this time. The sweethearts and wives of the boys from all parts of the state swarmed about the station to say good bye. There were lots of mothers and fathers too. The sweethearts smiled but the mothers and wives shed tears. I saw a few tears in the eyes of some of the married men. It made me think of the song I have heard father sing so many times. Here are two lines: "Go watch the foremost ranks in danger's dark career; Be sure the hand most daring there, has wiped away a tear." There were a thousand handkerchiefs fluttering in the air waving final adieus as the two long trains bearing the 25th slowly pulled out of the station to begin their journey south. I don't remember what I wrote you about Cairo. They say it is a bit like Cairo in Egypt. Our Cairo has more rats I'll bet, and it is built right in the forks of

---

1. Now Gilmanton, Buffalo County, Wisconsin. [*Wisconsin Magazine of History*]

the Ohio and the Mississippi rivers. I don't like the people. They are half rebs, never look at a soldier nor speak in passing. There are a lot of steamers tied up here loaded with supplies for Vicksburg and other points occupied by our troops.

The site of our camp here in Columbus, Ky. is fine. We can see for miles up and down the river. We are on a high bluff 200 feet higher than the town. The water is not good tho and we drink cold coffee to quench thirst. No enemy can approach us by water and on the land side we throw out pickets every day in a half-moon circle touching the river above and below town, so we cannot be taken by surprise from the land. We have a lot of heavy cannon behind strong breastworks overlooking the river so that no hostile fleet could reach us. On the land side there seems little danger of attack. Half the people in this part of Kentucky are Union and we would have plenty of warning of any rebel advance. I have been on picket duty in the woods some two miles from town twice since coming here. My beat was supposed to keep moving constantly back and forth for two hours at a stretch.

A comrade would be on a similar beat either side of me but one was not allowed to have any conversation with comrades on guard. Say I want to tell you its a lonesome job specially if the night is cloudy and dark. Its an awful good time to think of home and soft warm bed and all that. Then I would say to myself—what's the use. When the stars are shining I always look for the dipper and the north star. They are both a little lower down here than in the North but they look just as friendly as they did in Wisconsin. There is a sort of companionship in the stars when one is alone. I remember how I used to look up at the stars when I was out trapping alone with old Prince, over Traverse Creek or in Borst Valley. The barking of foxes and the snort of passing deer would keep me awake for hours. Old Prince and I slept under the same blankets with nothing over us but the sky.

Ah, but those delightful days are no more and I am here in far away Kentucky. Confound it there goes the drum. It means put on your belts and get out for drill.

Good bye,
Chauncey

Columbus, Ky., March 5th. 1863.
25th Wis., Vol. Infantry

Dear Folks at Home:

I sent you a letter a day or two ago and maybe I will hear from you soon. I hope I shall. I am well and we are hearing and seeing things and the days are not so heavy as at Madison. The weather is fine—most of the time warm and clear.

We drill every day, do police work, cleaning round the camp, and take a stroll now and then back in the country, far as the pickets will let us. We are really in the "Sunny South." The slaves, contrabands, we call them, are flocking into Columbus by the hundred. General Thomas of the regular army is here enlisting them for war. All the old buildings on the edge of the town are more than full. You never meet one but he jerks his hat off and bows and shows the whitest teeth. I never saw a bunch of them together but I could pick out an Uncle Tom, a Quimbo, a Sambo, a Chloe, an Eliza, or any other character in *Uncle Tom's Cabin*. The women take in a lot of dimes washing for the soldiers, and the men around picking up odd jobs. I like to talk with them. They are funny enough, and the stories they tell of slave life are stories never to be forgotten. Ask any of them how he feels and the answer nearly always will be, "Sah, I feels mighty good, sah," or "God bress you, massa, I'se so proud I'se a free man." Some are leaving daily on up-river boats for Cairo and up the Ohio River. The Ohio has always been the river Jordan to the slave. It has been the dream of his life even to look upon the Ohio River.

The government transports returning from down river points where they had been with troops or supplies would pick up free men on every landing and deliver them free of charge at places along the Ohio and upper Mississippi points.

The slaves are not all black as we in the North are apt to suppose. Some of them are quite light. Those used as house servants seem to have some education and don't talk so broad. A real pretty yellow girl about 18 was delivering some washing to the boys yesterday. She left her master and mistress in December and came to Columbus. In answer to the questions of the boys she said she left home because her mistress was cross to her and all other servants since Lincoln's emancipation. She said her mother came with her. One of the boys asked her why her father did not come with her. She said, "My father hain't no colored man, he's a white man." When the boys began to laugh she picked up her two-bushel basket of clothes, balanced it on her head and went her way. That girl must have made fifty stops among the tents leaving her basket of clothes. I wonder if she heard the same dirty talk in each of them. The talk wasn't clean, but some of us who tho't so just let it pass and kept still.

The talk now is our regiment will be divided—half sent up the Ohio to Ft. Donelson, the other half down the river. But this may be but one of many like rumors. There is always something in the air. Say but the picture before me as I write this is fine. I am sitting on the rampart of the Fort 200 feet above the river. The river, turbid and swollen from melting snows in Ohio and Indiana, boils and swirls as its mighty current strikes the bluff almost directly below where I sit. A regiment of cavalry has just landed from a government boat, and is climbing the bluff in a long winding column. The horses are fresh and they come prancing along, the swords of their riders jingling as if they were proud of their part in the scene. They don't know where they are going but doubtless to garrison some post farther south in the state. Wrote Ben Gardner some time ago, am afraid he has fallen or taken prisoner. He has always been prompt to answer. His regiment is south of Memphis.

I am afraid you will think me given too much to frequent and long letters, but I remember father's advice never to limit postage or letter paper expenses.

I should have mentioned that while the health of the boys is good in the main, we have some twenty in regimental hospital. Nathan Mann of our company and Orlando Adams of Mondovi are not expected to live.[2] These poor fellows are victims of the measles and were sick with me in the hospital at St. Cloud, Minn.

Direct as before to Columbus.

Your son,
Chauncey.

---

2. Nathan Mann died at Columbus, April 13, 1863. Orlando Adams was sent north but died in Grant County, Wisconsin, June 18, 1863. Charles Estabrook, *Wisconsin Losses in the Civil War* (Madison, 1915), 127, 130. [*Wisconsin Magazine of History*]

Columbus, Ky., March 10th 1863.
25th. Wis. Vol. Inft.

Dear Parents:

Rec'd a letter from home yesterday. It came to Columbus and was re-mailed to me at Cairo where our company had made a halt enroute with five other companies to Ft. Donelson. We stopped at Cairo to get our new guns. They are not here but we are going to wait for them. Cairo is not so muddy as when we came here in February. Still the water the river is 12 feet higher than the prairie behind the town. The levee or filling is all that saves the town from drowning.

I am sorry you are so frightened when you read of the big guns and stacks of cannon balls. I thought I had a more courageous mother. You know it is said that it takes ten ton of iron and lead to kill one soldier. Just think of that and take courage. They looked kind of ugly to me at first but now I never think of their being fearsome. We may have a different feeling about them when the time comes to use them. I stood guard last night on a government transport loaded with hardtack and sow belly. I never saw so many rats, the boat was swarming with them. Of course they had plenty to eat. I counted more than a hundred rat holes in the cracker boxes. The day before we left Columbus a steamboat tried to pass down by the fort without landing. She was hailed and ordered to land. It was found that she was loaded from St. Lewis with medical supplies, mostly quinine for the rebel forces at Vicksburg. Of course the boat and its cargo were confiscated.

I am glad you like your new team so well. I hope they will be all right. I shall want a cutter to match them when I get back so I can step round a little.

Say, mother, I had a question asked me yesterday by Elder Harwood, our Chaplain, that set me to thinking and stumped me so I couldn't answer. He asked me if I would go with him after the war. He said he wanted to get five or six good smart young boys that would go with him thru college. I answered that I could not say at once but would tell him later. Now mother, advise me what to say to him. The Elder is a minister of course, and altho he did not say, I suppose he meant to educate us for the ministry. Mr. Harwood is a mighty fine man and I like to hear him talk. He preached the other Sunday in one of the churches in Columbus, and in his prayer he thanked God for the freedom of the slaves. Some of the boys don't like this in him, but they are mostly the tough sort. I was in his tent when a colored woman brot his washing and he spoke to her as nicely as if she was a white woman. When she curtseyed and called him massa, he said, "My poor woman I am not your massa, you have no massa any more, President Lincoln has made all the colored people free just like the white folks." The poor woman kept saying, "Bress de Lord, bress de Lord, dis am de yeah of jubilee." When he handed her a fifty cent scrip to pay for the washing she looked at the picture of Lincoln on the corner of the bill, and putting it to her mouth, kissed it. The Elder asked her what she did that for, and she answered, "O bress you, honey, Massa Abraham Lincoln is de first and onliest Savior of us poor niggahs, an we des love dat face of his."

The order to go to Ft. Donelson has been recalled and we are to go back in a day or so to Columbus, I am glad of anything to get us out of these rat hole barracks. They run over our faces at night and we can't sleep. When I remember the talks of Elder Morse and father about the wrongs of the slaves, I wish they might be in Columbus a few days and see and hear them as I have.

Your son.
Chauncey.

COLUMBUS, KY., MARCH 20TH, 1863.
25TH. WISCONSIN VOL.

Dear Mother:

The six companies of our Regt. ordered last week to Ft. Donelson returned to Columbus last night after a week's stay at Cairo. Glad to get back to the top of the big bluff once more. We got here at midnight. There is an awful flood in the Ohio pouring into the Mississippi at Cairo from the melting snow above, and the seething water is black as mud. The air of our camp is fine compared to the miasma of Cairo. A short time ago I read a letter in the Alma *Journal* purporting to be a dream by S. S. Cooke. It suited the boys to a dot. Some of them tho't it was a daydream with his senses and eyes wide open. It seems you are still having winter weather. Grass here is fine picking for cattle and there is a lazy summer-like quietness in the air. The trees are leafing and the spring birds are here in force. I have seen several gray thrush in my strolls in the woods and strings of ducks and wild geese are passing north daily. Well if I was a wild goose I suppose I would go north too.

March 21st. After drill went out in the edge of the woods. Its more peaceful and homelike than the racket of the camp. I can see the picket guard beyond me slowly pacing his beat. There is no enemy about but the discipline and regulations are just as rigid as they are in Georgia. No white man can come within the picket line except he has the password. A negro is allowed to come in. We are afraid that the whites may be spies, we know that the blacks are our friends. The health of the regiment is good save a few cases of bowel trouble. The boys call it the Kentucky quickstep. There is more sickness among the poor lazy blacks. They are filling all the vacant houses and even sleeping under the trees, so anxious are they to get near de "Lincoln soldiers." They live on scraps and whatever they can pick up in camp and they will shine our shoes or do any camp work for an old shirt or cast-off coat. They had a revival meeting at the foot of the bluff last night and such shouting and singing and moaning. It was Massa Lincoln was a savior that came after two hundred years of tribulation in the cotton fields and cane. They had long known that something was going to happen because so many times their massa had visitors and they would tell the servants to stay in their cabins and not come to the "big house" until they were called. Then some of the house servants would creep round under the windows and hear the white folks talking about the war and that the slaves were going to be free. And when the one that was sent to listen would come back and tell the others, they would get down on their knees and pray in whispers and give thanks to the Lord. Everything with the darkies is Lord, Lord. Their faith that the Lord will help them has held out more than 200 years. I sometimes wonder if the Lord is not partial to the white race and rather puts it onto the black race because they are black. We sometimes get terribly confused when we try to think of the law of Providence. This black race for instance, they can't talk ten words about slavery and old Massa and old Missus, but they get in something about "de blessed Lord and de lovely Jesus" and yet in this land of Washington, God has permitted them to be bought and sold like our cattle and our hogs in the stockyards, for more than 200 years. I listened for two hours this morning to the stories of a toothless old slave with one blind eye who had come up the river from near Memphis. He told me a lot of stuff. He said his master sold his wife and children to a cotton planter in Alabama to pay his gambling debts, and when he told his master he couldn't stand it, he was tied to the whipping post stripped and given 40 lashes. The next night he ran to the swamps. The bloodhounds were put on his track and caught him and pulled him down. They bit him in the face and put out his eye and crushed one of his hands so he could not use it. He stripped down his pants and showed me a gash on one of his hips where one of the hounds hung onto him until he nearly bled to death. This happened in sight of Nashville, the capital of Tennessee. I told this to some of the boys and they said it was all bosh, that the niggers were lying to me. But this story was just like the ones in *Uncle Tom's Cabin* and I believe them. And father knows of things very much like this that are true.

I will write you again soon.

Your son,
Chauncey.

Columbus, Ky., March 25th, 1863.
25th Regiment Wisc. Vol.

Dear Father:

Your latest letter rec'd. I am perfectly happy to know that all are well at home. Don't worry about my morals or my health, I am taking pretty good care of both. The life of the soldier is not a very good reform school, but a boy can keep clean in the army, bad as it is around him, if he has the stuff in him. Our Lieutenant Colonel was talking about the loose ways of some of the soldiers the other day. He said there would be one man if he lived that would go home as clean as when he entered the army, meaning himself of course.

Dan Hadley got a letter from Geo. W. Gilkey the other day. It was a nice friendly letter. He said he hoped we would hurry up and lick the rebels so we could come home as they needed our society in Buffalo Co. He said the girls were all waiting for a soldier boy. Mr. Gilkey seems to be a fine man. I see by the northern papers there is talk of conscripting. Are you in the conscript limit? I hope not. I would hate to see you in the army. I don't think the government will need any more soldiers. They are planning a big campaign on the Potomac to try and break Lee's army. Grant has driven Gen. Pemberton into Vicksburg and is closing in around that city. The move seems to be to lay siege and starve him out. . . .

There are some rebel officers in prison here. I was on provost guard the other day and stood on a post near a barred window of the jail.[3] I could see four or five young-looking fellows in the room walking back and forth in their grey uniforms, trimmed in fancy gold braid and shoulder straps. They would call me up to the window and try to make snakes out of me. They said I was a black Republican and that I was fighting for the niggers and didn't know it. The oldest one talked like a gentleman, asked me a lot of questions about Wisconsin, and said he had a boy in the Southern army about my age.

Since the hot weather we are all getting our hair shaved off. Mine is cut close to my scalp. Boats are passing daily loaded with troops for Vicksburg. It begins to look warlike in that vicinity. There will be a big battle if Pemberton will come outside his breastworks and fight. We look any day for orders to go down there. We don't know the names of the troops that go by but we always give them a good big hurrah and they send it back with a roar.

We expect the 27th Wisconsin here tomorrow. We will make them welcome as we have a lot of picket duty for the force at this place. Yes I wish you would send me the *Sentinel* while we stay here at least. Northern papers are peddled in camp at from ten to fifteen cents apiece.

It's nice that you have some fresh cows. Better not try to raise the calves, you have so much else to do. We get pretty good milk from the nearby farmers but they don't know how to make butter. Its white and rank. The cows down here are a poor starved looking race. They have no grass for hay much to depend on, they have cornstalks for feed in winter. The Blue Grass region is away east of here. That is the home too of the Kentucky horses we have read about.

Well, the boys are putting on their belts getting ready for the call to drill, so I must close for this time.

Love to all,
Your son,
Chauncey.

---

3. The provost guard served under the direction of the provost marshal, whose responsibilities included internal policing of the army and maintaining order in areas of military occupation during the war. The provost marshal also oversaw recruiting. The provost guard was responsible for prisoners of war, and the provost marshal heard complaints from civilians regarding damage and loss of property and other injuries due to military activity. George McClellan created the office of provost marshal. [WM]

Columbus, Ky., 25th Regt.
April 10th, 1863.

Dear Mother:

Your much valued letter received. I am just as glad as I can be that all are well, but there is a tone of plaint as to things I can't understand. It must be you have the blues. Don't think of me as being in danger for a minute, for I am having a royal good time. Its this way with me. If I have the blues it is when I get a fit on of thinking of the past when I didn't do as I should. I guess you would call it remorse. Some of the younger fellows and I have talked these things over and I find they were kind of troubled in the same way. They said it made them feel awful mean when they remembered some sly things or some deception they played on their mother and father. These things bring on homesickness and that sends them to the hospital, because they can't eat and so are put down on the sick list. I think as much of home as any of them but I don't want to see it until we thrash the rebs to a finish. We have four Wisconsin regiments at this place, the 25, 27, 31 and 34, a full brigade. You have doubtless heard that the Governor is enlisting negroes and forming negro regiments. They are officered by whites and there are a lot of candidates for positions in all the white regiments. Some 25 have applied for positions from our regiment. There is a lot of joking on the side about the fellows that want to officer the nigger regiments. Our regiment has just drawn a new outfit of rubber blankets, hats and short coats. Enclosed you will find some flowers given me by a poor black washer-woman I met on the road up the bluff today with a bundle of clothes on her head. As she handed them to me she said, "Please massa will you 'cept dese flowers from a poor nigger woman who jes loves de Lincoln soldiers. Maybe you has a sweetheart and will send um to her." I told her I had a sweetheart, my mother, and she said "You's a good boy, honey." The black folks are awful good, poor miserable things that they are. The boys talk to them fearful and treat them most any way and yet they can't talk two minutes but tears come to their eyes and they throw their arms up and down and praise de Lord for de coming of de Lincoln soldiers.

In your last letter you spoke of my going to school, if I ever return. I am not bothering about things so far in the future. I am troubled about this awful war. Maybe I ought to think more of Webster, as father keeps jibing me about my spelling. If he will give me time I will learn to spell too as I ain't but 16 years old, that is I'll be 17 on the 15th of May if there has been no juggling with the family register.

By the way I nearly lost some valuables the other night. I was on provost guard, the other night in town, at the depot. My relief had lain down at 11 o'clock for a four-hour sleep. At 3 o'clock in the morning we were routed to go on guard. Feeling in my pockets I found my gold pen missing. My money I had placed in my shirt pocket was safe. The comrade next me lost $17. In the morning my gold pen and holder was found in the mud near the platform. A detective force has been looking for the thieves but they don't find any thieves. Word has just come that Nathan Mann of our Co. has just died in the hospital. Poor fellow, he has two brothers left in our company.

A skirmish yesterday at Hickman, 26 guerillas were captured and bro't to this place for confinement as prisoners of war. There is nothing very stirring about us. The boys are getting tired of mere guard duty and are hoping for any chance that will send us to the front. For my part I ain't dying to go to Vicksburg where there is a better chance of getting killed as some claim they are. Maybe they are more anxious to die for their country than I am but from what I know of them I am doubtful. There is nothing farther from my mind at this writing than a wish to die for anybody or anything. I am hoping and praying for anything to make the rebels squeal and call it quits so I can come home and have a good time. Of course I am willing to take my chance, come what may, but I would a little rather live, come what may.

Tell Elder Morse Henry is all right and eats, if any difference more than his rations every day.

Love to all.
Your son,
Chauncey.

HEAD QUARTERS 25TH REGT. WIS. VOL. INFT.
COLUMBUS, KY.
APRIL 15TH, 1863

Dear Father:

Yours of April 9th came in due time. I am so glad all are well and that you are so cheerful and hopeful that the war will soon end.

You must be very brave to undertake so much work as you have planned, this spring. I have just received a letter from cousin Ben Gardner, whose regiment is camped just back of Memphis, Tennessee. You know he is in the cavalry. He says he is orderly and having a good time. Plenty of rations, no bullets to face and regular pay. He says, "I hope to meet you my son and talk over family matters and get a good look at you." I'll bet he is a lively fellow and loves a good time. He writes about the war as if it was a picnic. I enclose his last letter. He has no fear of rebel bullets, you can see that.

We moved our camp yesterday over near the brow of the overhanging bluff. The view is much finer especially of the Mississippi. Say, father, do you know I never look at the river but I think of home. I go down to the shore nearly every day to wash my feet. When I dip my hand in the water I think that it comes from Wisconsin and I wonder what part of it came from Beef River. It is terribly black and muddy, made so by the water of the Missouri that flows into it above St. Louis. From our new camp we can see the daily mail boat, 12 or 15 miles away, that brings us good and bad news from home and from Washington.

Last night I lay awake for hours listening to the honk honk of the wild geese passing over our camp toward the north. Does the dam which we repaired, the beaver dam east, still hold? If it does you must have plenty of shooting at ducks and geese this spring. Don't think me homesick, father, when I tell you I turned over many times in my bunk last night thinking of the stories you told me of the early French traders who broke the great beaver dams to get the beavers and so destroyed the nesting places of the wild ducks and geese that made their homes in our valley and on the neighboring creeks before the coming of the whites. That novel called *The Prairie Flower*[4] still sticks in my craw. I never read any book that so haunted me, sleeping or awake. I remember that you told me that it was poison to read such stuff, but I don't believe it has hurt me. The people in *The Prairie Flower* were not in fear of any law but they did right in the midst of the Sioux Indians and the lonesome hills and wild animals about them. I remember you said "Prairie Flower" was a fictitious character, an unreal character, and that women were not as good on the average as she was painted. Well, father, I thought you might be wrong then but now I have come to think that you were right. Getting back to ducks and geese and the beavers,

---

4. *The Prairie Flower* was written by Emerson Bennett, a popular novelist of the period. Originally published in 1849, it was one of his most successful novels, selling some 100,000 copies. Like most of Bennett's novels, *The Prairie Flower* is a romantic treatment of the western frontier, with a sentimental and melodramatic plot, in this case involving a series of adventures among the Indians. Bennett was a very successful writer in his day, publishing more than fifty novels and hundreds of short stories. His popularity faded before his death in 1905. [WM]

how I wish I might be with you this spring. What lots of fun you are having. All this passed through my mind last night as I lay in my tent with the lappel thrown back so I could see the north star and the dipper. Both of them are nearer the horizon than in Wisconsin. But they brought to me in their silence and sameness something of the nearness of home.

The deep, dark forests on the Missouri side reaching back for miles are slowly turning to green. Spring is here and no mistake. The freshness of the grass and leaves, the golden sunshine and carol of birds in every tree, give no hint of this human war. One thing I most forgot. I expressed $20 with Capt. Dorwin to Durand. You may have to go to his home for it. His family lives about three miles from Durand. I have an overcoat I wish was home. I will give it away to the first darkey that looks like Uncle Tom. I know there are some greybacks in it. I would rather put the greybacks on some darkey than on mother, for I know she dreads such things.

I send you today a couple of Southern papers. One, *The War Eagle,* printed at this place, the other a Vicksburg sheet full of brag and bluster about fooling the Yankees. They are a fair specimen of Southern newspapers. Are there any copperheads up there? It makes the boys mad to read of copperheads at home. They are more dangerous than rebels at the front because the South is made to believe they have lots of friends in the North. They had better lay low if we ever get home. They will find its no joke to the South.

How I should like to have a brotherly tussel with brother K. and I think of the boys so often. Well, we will have a good time when the war is over.

How does Henry Amidon prosper? Confound him he has forgotten old times I guess. I have written him but he don't answer. I asked him in my letter if he remembered the time his father caught us down by the swimming pool laying in the hot sand stark naked and covering ourselves with the sand. I never was more ashamed in my life than when his father hollared and yelled to see us and we rolled into the creek to hide. Henry didn't mind it as much as I did. O, but those were happy days and we didn't know it.

Father, good bye till next week.

Your son,
Chauncey.

COLUMBUS, KY., MAY 3RD, 1863.
HD. QUARTERS, 25TH. WIS., VOL. INFT.

Dear Sister:

I am pleased that you have a good school and a good boarding place. That strapping boy so dull in his lessons may come handy in a fight with the others some time. Try and get home to see the folks often. Mother is worried for fear our regiment will be sent to Vicksburg where Grant is collecting a big army to storm the city. There are no rumors of our going of late, tho troops are passing down the river daily bound for Vicksburg.

So Ezra C. is writing home some dreadful tales of guns and drums and gory battles? Let me tell you a bit of a secret. I don't want to dispute anybody, but he has not fired a gun. His story of the groans of the wounded and dying and the din of battle does his imagination more credit than his sense of truth. I know where their regiment is posted and if they have been in any fights, the war department don't know of it.

Our Colonel has granted 100 furloughs to the regiment which means 10 men to each company. Those that are sick and convalescent will get the preference. I am glad I am not in either list of unfortunates. I am feeling fine. I believe I have recovered from every ill effect of the measles in Minnesota. Poor Orlando Adams of Mondovi is still down and may never get better. Orlando has applied for a discharge, but they are hard to get. I wish he might go home for he is a very sick boy, and some say there is no hope for him. John Le Gore and one or two Mondovi boys are going to get furloughs.

Some new war songs have struck camp lately. One of them is "When Johnny Comes Marching Home." The band boys tent, Chet Ide's headquarters, gets the new songs first. If there is anything funny about them, we can hear Chet laugh his peculiar hearty laugh. Another darkey song, "Babylon is Fallen," had been going the rounds. It begins, "Don't you see de black cloud risen ober yonder, whar de ole plantation am?" I was in a saloon down town yesterday with a lot of the boys, some darkies were singing it. I could have heard it all day. The boys would chip in a penny each and the black fellows sang it over and over. Then they got the negroes to butting. Alec Harvey gave five cents, I gave five, and a lot of others. The darkies would back off like rams and come together head to head. They said it did not hurt, but I believe it did. The boys kept setting them on by giving them 5 cent scrip. The darkies were kept about half drunk to give them grit.

I was on picket duty the day I got your letter, about two miles in the country. I went to a house near my beat and found a lot of Union girls, anyway they said they were for the Union. One of them asked me my age. When I told her she said that was just about her age. They gave me a lunch of corn bread and a piece of pork. When I came away I got some milk in my coffee can and a piece of Johnnie cake for 10 cents. I saw three blacks, two men and a woman working around. I don't know whether they were slaves or hired help. I am going to get a pass one of these days and go back and buy some of the old lady's butter. Of course I ain't thinking about the girls. I have lately found out there are a lot of fellows getting passes to go into the country for milk and butter that are lying like troopers. It ain't milk they want nor butter. They are looking for pretty girls or rich widows. Such things are common talk in the tents after the candles are lit until bedtime. Some of them have got so far in their fancies that they say they are coming back to Columbus after the war is over.

By the way, have you got that box of clothing yet? You say nothing about it.

I often think of you and father singing together the plantation songs of the slaves. But do you know I would give O, so much if you could have heard what I heard last night. A steamboat from St. Louis lay here at wharf last night waiting for orders. After unloading its freight, the deck hands, all darkies, joined in singing a lot of plantation songs. I sat on some cotton bales watching them and listening to their curious speech. They gathered on the forecastle of the boat and for more than an hour sang the most pitiful songs of slave life I ever heard. The negroes may not know much, but they sing the most sorrowful songs in the sweetest voices I ever heard. It is wrong for me to have wished you here to hear them, because you would have shed tears. Just before I left one of them came up the gang plank near me. I asked him how long he had been free. He said he quit his old massa in Tennessee last December and shipped on the steamer, *Natchese*, at Memphis. I asked him where he learned the songs he had been singing. He answered "I don't know, massa, cept de jes growed up wid me. Seems like I always knowed um. Maybe I learned um from my old mammy who used to sing um wid me fore she was sol' down in Alabama." As the poor black wretch shuffled along past me (he had no clothes above his waist) I noticed scars across his back as if made by a whip.

I paid 10 cents for a New York paper yesterday. It had a speech in it by Wendell Phillips on the horrors of slavery. I am just beginning to see what made father walk the floor and say hard things about the slaveholders after reading a speech by Wendell Phillips.

You will get this letter when you go home.
Death to copperheads.

Your brother,
Chauncey.

Columbus, Ky., May 12th 1863,
Hd. Quarters 25th Wisc.

Dear Mother:

At last we are under marching orders for the South. Hurrah. The orders came yesterday and I am just writing to tell you the glad news. I don't know why, but the boys are clear gone wild about it. They say they enlisted to fight and they want to fight. We have some rebel prisoners down town and they have been talking pretty saucy to the guard. They say one Butternut (that is the color of their uniform) is good for four Yanks. Poor ignorant devils. They don't know but little more than the negroes, they use the same brogue. If you shut your eyes you would think from their jargon you was talking to a lot of "niggers" as they call the blacks. A call for dress parade. I suspect some important order will be read. Will finish later.

May 13th. This morning we were relieved from further marching orders and told to resume our former quarters. Last night came a rush order to strike camp and march double quick to a boat lying at the wharf. I had just gone to bed like the others and was asleep. Orderlies were rushing from one tent to another calling the boys to up and dress and fall in. In ten minutes time or less every tent along the ten company streets was struck and the match applied to everything of bedding and bunk boards that would burn. Eck Harvey and Bill Anderson, the twins, as they were called, the two biggest men in the company, had just come up from town and were feeling pretty well. They were swearing and calling it a rebel scare. After everything was in a blaze and the companies lining up for orders a cavalryman came dashing along bound for the Colonel's tent. What did the messengers mean? Was it a countermanding order or was it a hurry order? The order came to return to camp, and the camp all in a blaze. Such a howl as went up from a thousand mad men you never heard. I am sure it must have looked to the hundreds of negroes who were watching us as if the devil with all his fireworks and his imps had come to Columbus. This is but one incident of that suspense peculiar to the life of the soldier.

Here we had packed up our movables and burned the rest, and it was midnight and dark but for the fire. We lay down and pulled over us for the rest of the night the tent cloth and we went to sleep and dreamed of home and of father and mother just the same.

While we were eating our breakfast our good Lieut. Colonel ordered us to lose no time in falling in without arms. We were in line in a twinkling and waiting for further orders. The colonel then told us that Gen. Hooker had won a victory and he wanted us to give three great big cheers and a lot of tigers. And they were loud and long. Before this letter reaches you, you will have heard of Hooker's victory. Old Hooker is a fox, Old Hooker is a coon, is the praise heard on every side. And he deserves it all if what we hear is true. I heartily wish he had the bloody 25th in his command. If he had I kind of think we would have a chance to work off some of our conceit and surplus patriotism. Though we never met the enemy it is our belief no thousand rebels ever stood in line of battle that could take our colors.

The 11th Missouri came through here yesterday from Clinton 12 miles from this place. They are a hard favored set of war worn veterans. They had seen service. I never saw in my life such a sight as followed in their rear. Such human beings, once slaves. Some were black as ebony with great pitiful, white, rolling eyes, and some nearly white and as pretty and polite as any woman I ever saw. I wonder mother if you ever thought what it is to be a slave, that is for the women, the mothers and daughters. I have thought it all out and I will tell you some time if I ever come home.

Some sardine of a scamp pulled the rope out of our flag pole the other day. Ten dollars was offered anyone who would climb the pole and put it in the pole again. As I write there is a daring fellow on the tip top of the pole putting the rope in the pulley. As Lieutenant Brackett has skipt, our orderly has been promoted to second lieutenant and our second to first lieutenant. Sergeant McKay of Mondovi takes the first sergeant's place and Adam Heinbeaugh of Mondovi comes in as 8th corporal. I think we have the best set of officers in the regiment. We have a bully captain even if he did try to resign at one time. Captain Dorwin is a real good man. I would rather go into battle with him than any other man on the job. He can't keep step to the music, but he aint to blame. It just happens there is no time or music about him. The boys make fun of him but they like him just the same.

The fellows that were promoted had to set up the beer, and the way some of the brave lads drank to their health was a bit saddening to see. Of course your son had to drink some beer, not to be out of fashion, tho to tell the whole truth he had joined the cold water society. My excuse is I was told I could drink cider, and I find I can't so I was deceived. But I promise you, mother, I have not touched a drop of whiskey nor will I while I am in the army. I have never forgotten the firm stand father took soon as he found he liked the taste of drink, and I never shall. I never took a swallow of beer but I felt as guilty as a thief. I wrote sister D. only the other day. Love to the boys and father.

       Your son,
       Chauncey.

COLUMBUS, KY. MAY 23RD, 1863.
HD. QUARTERS, 25TH WIS. INFANTRY.

Dear Mother:

  I sent you a long letter the other day but I forgot to mention my birthday. In fact I was not reminded of it until the day after but it has come and gone. I am sure if I had been at home my good mother would have reminded me of it in the shape of something good to eat. I don't know as I am any older feeling than I was two weeks ago and the future looks just the same. When I see an old person I never think of being that way myself. Maybe the Lord will perform a miracle and keep me young like the story in the Old Testament, but if he doesn't I am pretty well satisfied to be in this good old world. When I go back in the country, away from the sight of these big, black cannons sticking their muzzles through the portholes of the fort, and look up to the green of the trees, and hear the hum of the bees and the twitter of the birds, and see the peaceful quiet of the country, it is hard to realize that the country is being torn to pieces in a big war.

  Dear mother, I should have answered your last letter more promptly. I have written so many of late. I had almost forgotten I owed you one. You know it is said everything is fair in war, and I know you will excuse me.

  During the last four days we have been shading our tents with brush. I tell you we have been fixed up nice. Standing off a little ways one can hardly see the tents and it makes it so much cooler. Hot? Well I should remark. These May days in old Kentucky make everybody loll but the darkies and nobody thinks of them. The heat pretty near drove us out of the tents in mid day. We take turns going over to the hospital to fan the sick boys and brush away the flies. The doctors say the younger ones are dying of homesickness much as anything.

Some of my chums and myself have been skylarking out in the country of late and we have visited a lot of pretty Kentucky homes. In a good many of them I am sure they hated to see us come in. They might be Union people but they hate to see us talking to their slaves and the soldiers were a little saucy where they thought they were not wanted. We would hunt the strawberry beds and eat them too. We would call for milk, butter, apples, and other good things to eat. Most of these people we knew were our bitter enemies and some of the boys were afraid their bread was poisoned. We found some places where we were invited into the house and where the young ladies would smile and would talk to us about our homes. We knew these smiling young ladies might have been traitors and might have spies hidden away to hear what was being said. The dwellings or cabins of the slaves were mostly empty. Here and there we saw a few old negroes who chose to stay by Ol Missus and Masser to leaving their old Kentucky home to go out into a strange world. These old slaves were awful shy and always made some excuse to get away when we tried to talk to them. I suppose they were afraid Masser would see them. I often wonder where the poor blacks will go to find a home and something to eat. Those I have talked with say they are treated better now since they can run away without being chased by dogs.

We found a pretty country home the other day where the young lady took us out in her flower garden and gave each of us a bunch of flowers. I am sure her mother did not like to see us there. She had a cross look on her face and watched us thru the window as if she feared we might capture the girl and run away with her. When we went away one of the Durand boys told the girl he hoped to come back after the war and making the prettiest bow she said she hoped he would. When we went back to camp we told Chet Ide and Joel Harmon of Mondovi what a picnic we had and we all joined in and sang "Our Old Kentucky Home." I found out a strange thing lately, the darkies don't know anything about the song of "Old Kentucky Home," except as they have picked it up from hearing the whites sing it. I guess I must have thought it came out of some negro's heart. Anyway whenever I met a negro alone anywhere I always wanted to ask him to sing that song. Those I did ask would smile and grin and say "Massa, I don't know it." Their ignorance of the song gave me a curious feeling.

This is a long letter. I hope it will find you all well as I am and happy. Love to the boys father and sister Do.

Your boy,
Chauncey.

Columbus Ky. May 29th, 1863
Hd. Quarters 25th.

My dear Mother:

Your last letter came in due time, just two and a half days from the hour it was written. It must have been dated wrong. I got a letter from father the same day. It had been held up somewhere. I suppose the mail clerks get things mixed sometimes.

We are under orders to march on short notice. We don't know if it means to go south, north, east, or west. It means just one thing and nothing else—"be ready." A soldier can't find any fault and if he does he is put in the guardhouse or if on a march he is tied up by the thumbs.

We have cooked up five days' rations and are ready at the first note of command to fall in. I am in a mighty hurry and must make this letter brief. Just another word. One of my mates wants me to say a good word for him to sister D. He is a nice clean fellow and all right. His only fault is quite common, he don't think the black race is just human. I can't beat him in argument but I know in my heart he is wrong about these poor, wretched black people. You need not get excited, marching orders may not mean anything. We may not strike tents for a month yet.

May 30th. Was out last night where the evening gun, a black cannon, booms the hour of sunset. A man pulls a string called a lanyard and a roar that shakes the great bluff follows, and all this means sunset. I learned last night what it meant in French. I was standing near the big black cannon which stands almost straight above the river some 300 feet. A negro sweep doing police work, a fine looking mulatto, was idly leaning upon his shovel and staring at a passing boat. "What are you thinking about?" I asked. Taking off his dirty cap and bowing, he answered with a smile, "I kind' hates to tell you, but I was thinking of my jewlarke." I didn't know what a "jewlarke" was so I asked him. "Why Massa," he answered, "just a sweetheart," and then he told me his story, how he was a slave in Louisiana, how he came out as cook for his master who was a lieutenant in a Louisiana regiment, how his master's cavalry company was surprised by Union cavalry, was fired upon by our boys, how he fell down to make believe he was dead and when our boys came up, he jumped to his feet and came back to Columbus with our boys. He had been at work in the fort at Columbus ever since. Whenever he spoke he took off his cap. I asked him what he did that for. He said slaves had to do that in the South. I asked him if he was glad he was free and he said, "O yes Massa, I would be glad if I had my Kizzie wid me." The poor fellow took off his hat as he said this and slowly replaced it again. I am sure I saw tears in the fellow's eyes. The song of "Nellie Gray" came to my mind. It disappoints me that the negroes have never heard these songs. They stare at you when you sing them. While we were talking the gunner came, and fixing the lanyard pulled the cord with a jerk and with a mighty roar that sent a tremor thru the bluff and a black smoke that hid the river for a moment told us that the sun had set and the flagman at headquarters slowly lowered the stars and stripes. "Soliquasha," said my colored friend. "What do you mean by that?" I asked. That is French he replied meaning sunset. Here was a slave teaching me French. Mother do you know I asked myself this question, what right have I simply because I am white to be the master race, while this man knowing more than I should be a slave because he is black. He called himself a Creole; that is a negro born in Louisiana. He said he was born in a parish 50 miles from New Orleans. His master raised sugar and rice and they toted it on two-wheel carts to New Orleans where they sold it. His Massa's plantation was long side a live oak swamp that was full of deer, bear, and aligators. He said the "gaitors" warnt so bad as folks let on. "De niggers had a swimming hole in de bayou whar an old gaitor had raised a nest of young uns every year. In the winter the gaitors buried themselves like frogs in the mud. When they came out in the spring you could hear them bellow all night long." I don't know and I don't care whether this fellow was stuffing me or not. I was interested. Things he said about New Orleans and things he told me about his master's plantation away back in the swamps made me think of the story of *Uncle Tom's Cabin*. It looks as tho this war was to change all this. The South has had a mighty soft snap with darkies to do their work for a hundred years, while their masters have grown rich and insolent to us of the North. The papers don't say much about it but the truth is these slave-holders, these three hundred and fifty thousand chivalrous Southern gentlemen, who own some four million of poor ignorant fellows who pushed to the front and were mowed down by Union bullets don't know what they fighting for. Love to father, brother, and sister D.

Your son,
Chauncey.

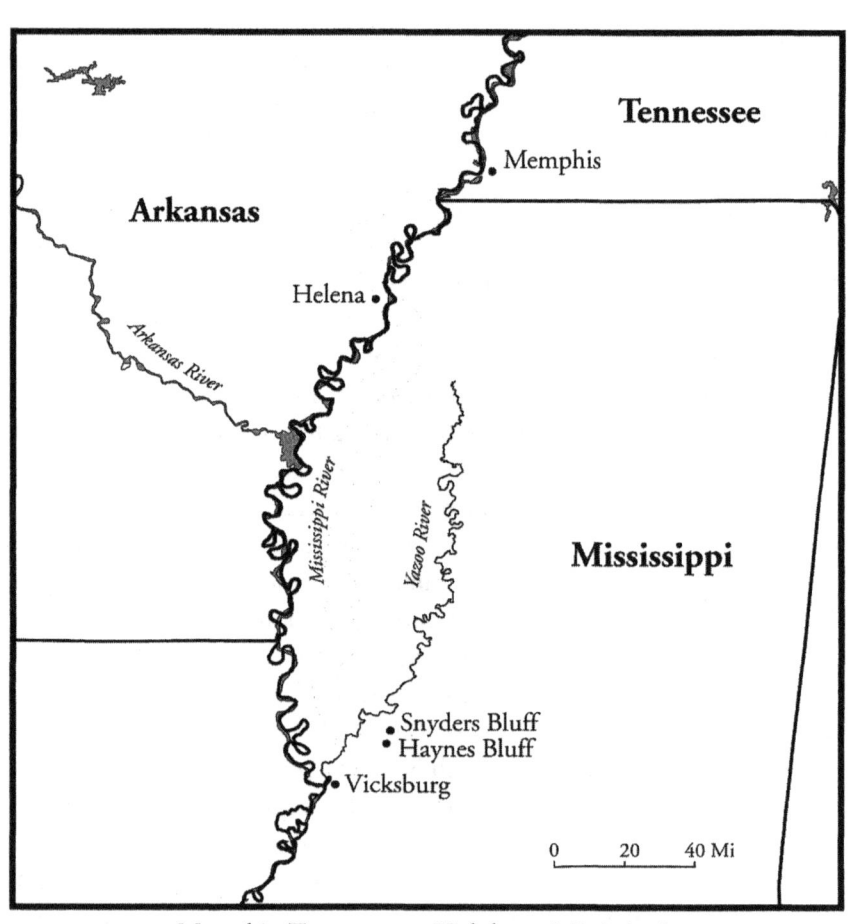

Memphis, Tennessee, to Vicksburg, Mississippi.
May 31, 1863–March 13, 1864.

THE VICKSBURG CAMPAIGN

Columbus, Ky. 25th Wis. Co. G.
May 30th, 1863.

Dear Folks at Home:
The final order came tonight after we had gone to bed, to be ready to go to Vicksburg by boat in the morning. There was a lot of skurrying around all the long night. Clothes at the washer-woman's had to be looked after. Letters had to be written as I am writing this by the dull light of a tallow candle, some to wives, some to mothers, fathers, and many to sweethearts. I hope there were no unhappy girls because of this sudden leaving near about Columbus. But I fear there was a few. I am quite sure of two or three. Well, I am content if we must leave Columbus even if it has been a sort of "Old Kentucky Home" to us for nearly two months. It is one o'clock in the morning and the lights are yet burning in the tents. In a lot of the tents they are singing the "Old Kentucky Home." I guess the boys don't think much of its meaning but sing it because we are in Old Kentucky. A lot of colored women are running about the tents collecting washing bills. They all seem to know that we are to leave in the morning. There will be a lot of unpaid washing bills, but the darkies won't mind it much as they are used to working for nothing.

Max Brill, my bunk mate, has finally shut his mouth, so has Delos Allen and John LeGore, my other tent mates, leaving me to blow out the light and go to sleep. Will finish letter and mail it in the morning.

May 31st. When we woke up this morning we found a great big New Orleans side-wheel packet lying at the wharf waiting to take us on board. The roll call found many of us still asleep after such a night. Many of the boys fell in for roll call in nothing but shirts and drawers. I got on all but my pants and shoes. About half the company was in the same plight. The orderly was so good natured we gave him a good long cheer and ran back to our tents to finish dressing. The town was crowded with country people, mostly colored folks, to see us leave. The grand march to the boat began at ten o'clock and it was near three p. m. when we were all packed away on the three decks. Our company was on the hurricane deck. When the black deck hands loosened the four inch cable that tied our ship to the shore, the Regimental band began to play Dixie. The big boat floated out into the current, the big propelling wheels turned round and round in the muddy waters, and looking back at the big high bluff which had been our home so long we did not know whether to be glad or sorry that we were leaving it.

There were hundreds to wave us goodbye, yes thousands. There were loud cheers and good wishes from the regiments we left behind. The blacks were afraid to come out in the open to show their good feeling but down by the river bank and from behind houses and fences where they could not be seen by the whites, they threw up their caps and hats and danced like crazy. The women caught their skirts with both hands and bowed and courtesied and some dropped upon their knees and held their hands above their head as if they were praying. The boys didn't seem to notice it much because they were niggers, but it made me think of some things in *Uncle Tom's Cabin*. I take one last look at Columbus and the fort on the bluff with the big black cannon peering out over the river. We make a bend in the river and Columbus is hidden from view.

A lot of boys are gathered on the forecastle singing "My Old Kentucky Home." I suspicion the fellows have a homesick streak on, they sing with so much feeling. Hickman is in sight but four miles away. I must close this line in order to mail it there. Those lines of Charles McKay I have heard father quote so often come to mind, "Groaning, steaming, panting, down the Mississippi."

Your son,
Chauncey.

HAINES BLUFF, JUNE 8, 1863.
25TH WIS. VOL.

Dear Father and Mother:

I've seen some tough hours the last three days, but am feeling pretty well at this writing. Every night the last three or four nights we have been laying on our arms, expecting the bugle call to fall in for battle. The nights are hot and sultry and we lay with nothing but the sky for covering. You know how warm it is in Wisconsin in June but O, Lord, it is nothing to Mississippi. Corn with you is about six inches high. Here it is four feet higher than a man's head. I never saw such big corn. While we lay at Satartia the boys went wild raiding and foraging the country for anything they could eat or wear or destroy, and it was all right, for every white man and woman was ready to shoot or poison us. The negroes were our only friends, and they kept us posted on what the whites were doing and saying. Their masters told their slaves that the Yankees had horns, that they eat nigger babies, and that they lived in the North in houses built of snow and ice, and that the Yankee soldiers were fighting to take the niggers back north where they would freeze to death. It is a fright what stories the whites tell their slaves. The younger ones know better and laugh when they speak of it, but some of the real black ones just from Africa look nervous and scared when the boys crowd around them to tease and play tricks on them. They seem to know what the boys want. They bring in chickens, turkeys, eggs, molasses, sugar corn pones, smoked meat, and honey. The boys don't treat them right. They cheat them out of a lot and their excuse is they stole the stuff from their white masters. The poor black creatures never get mad but just smile and say nothing.

The day before we left Satartia some of our boys raided a big plantation, took everything in sight, and came into camp with a mule team and wagon loaded with a fancy piano. They put the piano on board a steamboat and blindfolding the mules, which were wild, turned them loose in camp. It was a crazy thing to do. There was some bee hives in the wagon full of honey and bees. The mules ran over some tents nearly killing a lot of soldiers and scattering bees and boxes along the way. It was fun all right for some of the boys got badly stung.

June 8th.—We have been resting on our arms all day awaiting a report from couriers who are watching the rebel General Johnston. He has a big force and his plan seems to be to cut off our march to Haines Bluff where we would be in touch with the main Union army. In the afternoon we were ordered in line as were all the regiments of the three brigades. We were told the rebel army was moving our way and to be prepared at any moment.

June 9th.—We lay upon our arms all night. It was not a good night to sleep. We expected every hour an order to fall in and retreat to Haines Bluff. It came at daybreak. We had scarcely time to make coffee and fry hard-tack. Mounted orderlies with clanging sabers were rushing about with orders from headquarters. They would spring from their saddles leaving their horse in charge of a black servant, who always met them hat in hand at the Colonel's tent. Since daybreak there has been a fearful booming of cannons toward the south. All sorts of rumors are flying about. One is that Johnston has jumped in on our flank at Snyder's Bluff with his army and another report is that Grant has stormed the city of Vicksburg under cover of all his big guns.

If nothing happens will write in a day or two.

Your son,
Chauncey.

Haines Bluff, Mississippi.
Hd. Quarters 25 Wis., June 11, 1863.

Dear Sister:

Am in receipt of your last letter but an hour ago. You do write a good letter. So full of news, just the stuff for a brother in the war to read, and you tell things in such a good way. It's just like a story in a book. You are father's girl all over just as mother has often said. How I wish I could have some of the fish you tell of catching, only I don't like the fellow that took you home that time. He is nice looking and knows how to say pleasant things, but he is what our chaplain calls a roue. Look in the dictionary and see what roue means. I don't want my sister to keep company with a roue, if I understand the word. Let me tell you, my dear girl, most young men ain't as good as they ought to be. And I wish you would be more careful and mind me a little if you are older than I. But I must tell you of things here.

We had a dreadful march from Satartia to reach this place. It was a killing march. Our Division General was a coward, and the march began at sunrise and ended at ten o'clock that night. It was a retreat, a perfect rout. The rebel Johnston was supposed to be close in our rear with a body of Cavalry and the orders were to press forward with all possible speed. Through great forests and cornfields without end standing above our heads, in the hottest sun I ever felt, the army became a regular mob, every man for himself. Men threw aside their coats and blankets, their testaments and their shirts. Hundreds lay down in the corn rows, under the trees, and on the banks of the creeks, many of them in the faint of a sunstroke, others fanning themselves or cursing those in command. The constant roar of besieging mortar and cannon at Vicksburg grew louder and louder as we advanced. The ambulances and the ammunition and supply wagons that followed were full of men unable to march, long before night. You know that father always said I was mother's boy because I never was tired or never sick till I went into the army. It was about 4 o'clock in the afternoon, I had lost sight of every man of Company G, and was marching with a bunch of Indiana boys. I had divided the water with them I had in my canteen. I had thrown away a woollen shirt, and torn my blanket in two and left a part of that to lighten my load. My cartridge box was the heaviest thing we had, every man was loaded with all the bullets he could carry, for we expected to need them. I was just about fainting with the heat when one of the Indiana boys said, "My boy you better lay down, your face is awful red." We were on the bank of a muddy creek. I walked away from the road up among the trees and after taking a drink from the creek I lay down in the shade of a tree with no one in sight and fell asleep.

When I opened my eyes the sun was down and it was just getting dark. For a minute I didn't know where I was nor what had happened. Then the march and the mix-up of the day all came back to me. Here and there I could see through the woods the light of the camp fires. I went back to the road where I left my Indiana friends five hours before. I sat down while a battery of six guns went by, each drawn by six big horses. Then followed a rear guard of five or six hundred cavalry whose sabers and carbines clanged as they rode by. I knew if Johnston was so near, these cannon and cavalry would not be passing toward Vicksburg in this peaceful way. A straggling group of infantry followed the cavalry and I joined them. I had gone but a few steps when I felt a hand upon my shoulder. Turning to see who it was, what was my delight to see the Captain of my company, Captain Dorwin, smiling upon me. Like myself he, too, was lost from the company. The Captain had never looked so good to me. He had lain down by the road like me, overcome by heat, and he was anxious to find the company. Until I found Captain Dorwin I was ashamed to think that maybe I was the only one lost from the company. The Captain is a great big strong man and nice looking. And when I found the heat had played him out just as it had me, I took courage. After calling at about a hundred camp fires and half as many regiments we found our company and our regiment. If there is a just God he will punish the man that ordered that awful march. It was useless and uncalled for. We hear that the General has been arrested and will be tried by Court Marshal. Every soldier on that horrid march hopes he will be punished.[1]

The air is sickening with the stench of decaying flesh. Mississippi is full of cattle running wild in the cane brakes, and the boys are shooting great, beautiful steers as they would rabbits, leaving everything but the choicest parts on the ground to smell and stink. Ten miles from here the people in Vicksburg are starving for beef to eat and where we are camped the air is poisoned with the decaying flesh of animals more then we can eat. What a world this is. I am only giving you a brief sketch of the important things. Just think of the horror of 50,000 people with half enough to eat, with no rest nor sleep, stormed at with shot and shell, night and day, in the city of Vicksburg. They have dug holes under their houses and in the bluffs and on the river side to get away from the shot and bursting shell of Union guns. They can't get anything more to eat outside the city so they eat horses and mules to keep alive. O, but the poor wretched whites that let the rich slaveholders drag them into this war. The negroes tell us the rich white man in the South looks down on the poor white trash who has no slaves, as much as he does on the black man. And the common soldier in the rebel army is awful ignorant. There ain't one in ten that can read or write, and they think the Dutch boys in our army were hired in Germany and came over just to fight them.

I have just been notified by the Orderly Sergeant that I am to go on picket duty to-morrow and to put my gun in order. The reports that we get every hour from the pickets, that men are being shot, remind us that we are not in sleepy old Columbus, Kentucky, any more, where we could go to sleep without danger, except from the officer of the guard. I'll let you know in a few days how nice it is to do picket duty in the cane brakes of Mississippi within gun shot of the enemy's line. I haven't the least fear of danger, sister, and I am feeling real good after a two days' rest of racket and roar of big guns that put me to sleep nights and waken me in the morn-

---

1. The march here so feelingly described was far more fatal in its consequences to the regiment than any battle in which it was engaged during the war. Toward the end of July the regiment moved up the river to Helena, where for a long time it was practically prostrated by disease. Thus on August 16 the daily report showed but ninety men fit for duty. This condition is attributed by Quiner (*Military History of Wisconsin*, 736) to the "hardships of the recent rapid march from Satartia to Snyder's Bluff," to which was added the influence of the unhealthy location of the camp at the latter place. The table of Wisconsin regimental losses in the war significantly concludes the story: "The Twenty-fifth Regiment had 376 men die of disease, a far larger number than any other Wisconsin regiment suffered." [*Wisconsin Magazine of History*]

ing. There is an army of some 15,000 men around us and between here and Vicksburg. Love to all, father, mother, and the boys.

P. S.—There is a rumor at this moment that we are to counter march for Satartia to-morrow. I'll bet it is a false rumor.

Your brother,
Chauncey.

HAINES BLUFF, MISSISSIPPI.
JUNE 15, 1863.

Dear Father:

I sent sister D. a letter some days ago and promised to tell her something of picket duty close to the enemy's line next time I wrote. I made some notes in my memorandum every evening so I enclose them.

June 10th, 6 o'clock p. m. Have just come in from the picket line where I have been for four hours during the day, from ten to twelve this morning and from four to six this afternoon. Will go on again tonight at 10 o'clock for two hours and again at four o'clock in the morning until six.

It has been a blistering hot day, but I have kept in the shade of some great trees most of the time. My beat is about as far as from the house to the creek, on a ridge, something like the little hill behind the house. The soldier whose place I took this morning, belonged to the Jersey Zouaves, told me it would be nice during daylight, but to look out to-night. He said he had seen the glint of a gun barrel last night in the edge of the cane brake. He advised me to keep my eyes peeled and stay as much as possible in the shadow of the trees. I asked him how I could do that and obey orders to keep pacing his beat. He said I don't give a damn for orders when I am alone here at midnight, and the officer of the guard asleep in his tent miles from here. One thing he said, you will hear a lot of hogs grunting in the cane brakes. Maybe they are hogs and maybe they ain't. Some of the boys have been shot by those hogs so look out. These Jersey Zouaves are supposed to be dare-devils, simply afraid of nothing. They wear fancy uniforms covered with yellow braid and all sorts of yellow stripes. The rebel soldiers hate these Zouaves and try to shoot them wherever they can. They are toughs picked up from the prisons and jails of the cities. Nothing happened worth mentioning during the day. From my beat I could see the Yazoo River and miles of cornfields on the west now tramped down and ruined. On the east where the enemy line extends are deep forests and dense cane brakes. All day long hundreds of men, yes thousands, were chopping down the trees, felling them toward the enemy, and sharpening the limbs so that they would be hindered and at the mercy of our guns if they tried to charge our lines.

Columns of smoke from burning buildings fill the sky, and this afternoon a south wind brought the smell of smoke from the big cannon that keep up their awful roar about Vicksburg.

June 12th, 9 o'clock a. m. After a rather wakeful night we are back to quarters in camp and while waiting for coffee to boil will jot down a note or two. The air about the camp smells better this morning. Several hundred carcasses of cattle left to rot in the sun were buried yesterday. The smell had got to be terrible. I remembered what the Zouave told me when I went on guard last night and I kept my eyes wide open, and my ears too, during the two hours of midnight. I heard some rustling in the cane thicket on my left but the sound seemed to recede rather than come nearer so I concluded it was some animal. I don't think I was afraid the least bit, until midnight the boom of cannons at Vicksburg and the half circling fiery curves of the shells and the sudden lighting of the sky when they burst gave me something to see and to think of. From four till six this morning the firing at Vicksburg had nearly ceased.

June 14th. A letter of May 23rd from home to-day. I am glad as ever a boy could be, who is in love with his home. I had wondered why no letter came. I wish father had sent me some stamps. Money won't buy them here. They seem to forget my request for stamps. Saw D. D. Loomis yesterday, of the Second Cavalry. Sam, as they call him, is in good health and spirits. He is a sort of an assistant to the Commissary, looking after the horses and rations. The 8th Wis. too, is here. It still carries the Eagle.[2] The order for our return to Satartia up the Yazoo has been recalled. I am glad. The fact is, too many of our Regiment were beat out on the march here. There are nearly 300 men under the doctor's care as a result of that 35 mile march. If the water was good we would be happy. Blackberries are plenty and nice. Our Regiment went out last night three miles to support a battery planted on a ridge. We lay on our arms all night without being disturbed by the rebs. This place will be retaken by the rebels if possible.

---

2. This was "Old Abe," probably the most famous mascot in American military history. For an account of him see "The Story of Old Abe" in this magazine, II, 82–84. [*Wisconsin Magazine of History*]

Every precaution is being taken to secure it against attack. Johnston and Bragg are on their way here with an army to drive us out, but Old Rose, that is Rosecrans, is following them and we ain't afraid. How many troops we have here, I don't know, but somewhere between twenty and forty thousand. To drive us from here will cost the rebs a good lot of blood, and they know it. This is an easy country to fortify, just about as hilly as Buffalo County and the sides of the hills ten times harder to scale, because of the timber we have fallen against the enemy and dense jungle of canebrakes. It's nearly impossible to get through a Mississippi cane-brake. Here is where our fish poles come from.

There has been a lull in the firing at Vicksburg. There is a rumor that the Confeds have made a breach and are retreating up the Black River. Another story is that Jeff Davis is inside the City and Pemberton has asked a parley with a view to surrendering. Everybody is looking toward Vicksburg and wondering why the thunder of the guns has stopped. Another rumor says General Grant has mined their forts and has given them twelve hours to surrender and if they refuse the chain of forts will be blown up.

Have just heard that poor Orlando Adams, my chum from Mondovi, is dead. He tried to get a furlough but failed. I was afraid when I bid him goodbye in Columbus, Kentucky, I should never see him again. The poor fellow cried when we left him to go south. Orlando never recovered from the effect of the measles. He wanted so bad to go home to die, but the rules had been strict against furloughs. Big Bill Anderson of Durand has just peeped in my tent and asked about my health. He gave me some blackberries. He said he had been out foraging for the sick boys. Bill is a wild fellow, but he has a great big heart and I know he is sicker this minute than some of the boys he is nursing.

You may send this letter over to sister D.

Your son,
Chauncey.

SNYDER'S BLUFF, MISS.
HD. QUARTERS 25TH. WIS. VOL. INFT.

Dear Father:

Since my last letter we have moved our position to within eight miles of Vicksburg. Yesterday eleven regiments of Burnside's corps landed. The old fellow himself with his well-known side whiskers came also. His men think he is pretty near a god. The hills and valleys for miles and miles are literally white with tents, and the music of bands from morning till night is ringing in our ears. I think it would be safe to say there are not less than twenty-five thousand tents within a circumference of eight miles. Clouds of dust from moving troops fill the air in every direction. Several batteries of artillery are just passing, six to eight big horses to each gun, and the men riding on the cassions are breathing a constant smudge. They don't have to walk, that is one thing in their favor, but I don't think I would like the battery service.

Rumor is still in the air that the Rebel General Johnston is maneuvering to cut his way through to help General Pemberton in Vicksburg. That is the reason for so many batteries and infantry coming here and taking positions at this time. I am sure a hundred thousand rebels could not break our lines at this point. We have three lines of heavy fortifications with batteries every eighty rods. Several thousand spades are kept constantly busy strengthening the lines. Our regiment was out yesterday on spade duty. I suppose we did a lot of digging, but for my part I don't think I did more than an hour's work, and I am sure I worked as hard as anybody. It takes the darkies to dig. One hundred negroes will shovel as much dirt as a thousand yankee soldiers, and sing plantation songs all the time. I went out a mile yesterday on the second line to see them work and hear them sing. Most of their songs are love songs, and it's always something about the cotton and the canefields. Rules are mighty strict and getting stricter everyday. Our main work is to clean and polish up our guns, and to see that our cartridge and cap boxes are kept dry. We have inspection of arms every day at ten o'clock. Every gun is examined and woe to the soldier whose gun is not in order. We know not at what hour, day, or night the roll of the drum will call us into line of battle.

I noticed in a copy of the Alma *Journal* you sent me that the people of Gilmanton, had been subscribing funds for the U.S. Sanitary commission. The object is a noble one and I am glad the Gilmanton folks have gone into their pockets to help it. By the way does Mr. G. say anything more about the hundred dollars he was to donate toward a private school in our valley when I enlisted? Don't say anything about it. If he gives it, all right. If he don't, all right. I don't care for his hundred dollars. But of course as he volunteered to give it I never can think as much of him for lying about it. This sanitary commission is a soldier's home or stopping place, wherever a soldier happens to be, in any town in the north. He is given a bed and meals free of charge and medicine and care if he is sick. They are in the border states as well, too, where our troops are in possession. If they are out of money they can stay weeks or months without cost until they get money or transportation to go on.

Of course the good people of Gilmanton expect to celebrate the 4th of July and I expected to be with them when I enlisted but I shall not be there. I am glad to hear you say that my spelling is better than it was, although you don't find my writing any better. You say I don't write any plainer than Horace Greeley. Well, there were some that managed to read Greeley and what the world found in his writings makes me rather glad that my penmanship is no better than his.

I am glad that sister D. secured a school. She don't write me so often any more. What's the matter with her? If the folks at home could know what happy fools it made of us to get letters, they would write more of them and longer ones. I have half a mind to confess that I have had the blues for a couple of days. I have had a touch of intermittent fever. Hundreds of the boys are under the care of the doctor for chills and fever. We are drinking water a little better than poison, and the miasma of this Yazoo River is getting in its work. The cannonading about Vicksburg is fiercer than ever. Last night the doctor gave me some infernal stuff for my fever that kept me awake. It must have been midnight before I got to sleep. I lay with the flap of my tent thrown back watching the shells from a hundred mortars, making a fiery half-circle as rising like a flaming rocket, they circled and fell into the city; then followed the explosion. How can those people sleep? I should think the people of that city would be perishing for sleep. There has not been an hour the three weeks past but shells have been bursting in every part of the city.

There was a bunch of about fifty rebs passed our camp yesterday taken at Vicksburg in a charge upon our works. They were put upon a boat at this landing for transportation to the North. They tell awful tales of hunger and want of sleep in Vicksburg. It takes half the people all the time to put out the fires started by our shells and they have no flour and only horse and mule meat. They hinted that Jeff Davis was inside the lines. The story isn't believed but everybody is talking about it. It pleases me that Elder Morse likes my letters. I told Henry what his father said about his writing and he merely laughed. Henry Morse is sick at this time with chills and fever. It is a common sickness on this Yazoo River.

There is talk that the city will be stormed from the entire ten miles of line this week. A victory here and the surrender of Pemberton would open the Mississippi to the Gulf, then hurrah for Virginia and a healthier climate.

Send me some stamps as money won't buy stamps down here. Tell mother when I come back I'll bring her an aunt Dinah or a Topsy to show her how to bake hoe cake in the fireplace and roast potatoes in hot ashes.

Love to all,
Your son,
Chauncey.

Hd. Quarters 25th Wis. Vol.,
Snyder's Bluff, Miss., July 1, 1863.

Dear Father:

It has been some time since writing you last, but we have had a busy time coming and going and maneuvering; that is our regiment has been on the move for more than a week and no chance to write a letter nor to mail one. A week ago yesterday our regiment got orders to go to Cypress Bend, on the Arkansas side of the river, 200 miles up the river to capture or disperse a band of guerrillas that were firing from ambush along the shore on the passing steamers, trying to kill the pilots and cripple the boats. They have even fired into hospital boats that were flying hospital flags. Every able-bodied man in our regiment, about six hundred, was ordered into line, guns and ammunition inspected. The next morning we boarded the *Dexter*, a Mississippi boat that reached nearly across the Yazoo River, and were soon pushing down toward the father of waters. The idea of riding on the Mississippi again and heading toward home made us happy. And we figured on having a good drink soon as our boat touched the muddy waters of the big river that we somehow loved just because it flowed by our homes.

We had just been paid off for two months and the boys had a good fill of oysters and store crackers. I only got six dollars though. I had drawn some extra clothing and my little thirteen dollars was cut to three dollars a month. It was so long ago I got the clothes, I began to think the clothes were forgotten. Uncle Sam's paymasters have a good memory. Just as I am writing this the *Silver Moon*, a Yazoo steamer, is passing up the Yazoo toward Haines' Bluff. She has a caliope and it is playing "Nellie Gray." She is loaded with hard-tack and bales of hay clear to the water line and her half naked deck hands lying around on the hay bales look like so many alligators. She gave us the right of way and we pushed on down this river whose water though clear and tempting we dared not drink. The boys kept cracking away at the alligators that lay on logs and driftwood on the sand banks. The scaly things would flounder into the water and sink out of sight. Some of them looked to be seven or eight feet long, more of them were three or four feet.

We reached Young's Point in the evening and waited there all night for some cavalry and a battery that was to accompany us. We were just out of cannon range of Vicksburg. I lay on the hurricane deck of our boat and with my head bolstered up on my knapsack so I could see. I watched the fire of our gun boats in sight of us down the river as broadside after broadside was poured into the city. Every discharge would come up the river like a great roll of thunder. It may seem strange to you but all the first part of that night I was thinking more of home than of the things going on around me. It seemed as if the shells from the mortars went up into the clouds a half mile and then would drop in a circle of fire into the city of Vicksburg. They looked like meteors only their track was red and they would often burst before they reached the ground. I don't think I got to sleep before midnight and when I woke up the sun was shining.

June 26th. Our battery and cavalry regiment came at nine o'clock and at eleven o'clock we swung into the great river with bow headed up stream. Soon as we got fairly into the current the boys made a rush for the boiler deck to get a drink of the water that came from the lakes and springs of Wisconsin and Minnesota. It was dirty and muddy and we saw dead mules and cattle floating by and knew that it was the sewer for all the filth of the northern states, but whether we were dry or not we drank, and drank, until it ran out of our nose just because it came from the glorious North.

Well, all that day as we steamed up the great river we lay round and talked, dreamed, and loafed. There was scarcely a break in the deep dark forests that came right down to the river bank. Our guns were loaded and we had them in hand all day because we were warned that we might be attacked at any moment. We had in our fleet four transports loaded with troops, and three gunboats with heavy brass cannon.

June 27th. The weather is awfully hot. We are tied up at Cypress Bend where all the attacks have been made on passing vessels. Our boats are tied to the Arkansas shore. We had a rain last night that gave us on the top a good wetting but the air this morning is cooler for the rain. The gun boats anchored amid stream and sent a lot of shells over into the woods beyond the plantation that lies along the shore. The idea was to draw the fire of the rebel forces, but nothing came of our firing. The cavalry was landed at noon and deployed as scouts across the big bend in the river. At seven o'clock we ran to the Mississippi side and tied up for the night. Everything was quiet for the night. There were some boats calling to our guards as they passed during the night to find out if the river was clear to Vicksburg. Next morning we went on shore, both cavalry and infantry under cover of our gun boats. They first sent a few shells screaming through the tree tops a mile or two inland as a sort of feeler, but getting no reply the batteries, cavalry and infantry went ashore.

This letter will be finished next week.

CYPRESS BEND, ARKANSAS,
JULY 2ND, 1863.

Dear Father:

We deployed a good half mile in line soon as we got ashore in a grove of timber that lay between the river bank and the mansion of the planter and the village of negro huts that flanked the big house on the right and left. This plantation worked nearly 500 slaves we were told. The mansion was built on piers like most homes of the South, ten or twelve feet above the ground; the basement surrounded by a lattice and serving as kitchen and laundry and living place for the house servants. We had orders to make a careful examination of the place as it was thought the guerrillas we were after had made this place their headquarters. I was among the first to reach the house. There were no whites in sight but I saw a few scared-looking black faces who got out of sight as we came near. Some of the boys had talked with the blacks who denied that there had been any rebels quartered there. We knew the negroes were lying. We found where there had been beds and lots of ash heaps where there had been camp fires and the tracks of horses and scattering corn fodder. Five or six of us went to the stairway and opened the door leading on to the gallery. Just as we stepped in the wide hall, three women, an old grey-haired lady and two young ladies, came up to us and asked us not to come into the house. The oldest one pleaded pitifully, wringing and rubbing her hands first one and then the other, and then reaching out her hands toward us as far as she could urging us to stay out, all the while crying and at times screaming as if her heart was breaking. She said her mother was sick and likely to die and begged us to go away. I never felt meaner in my life. The Co. K. man who did the talking told her we had orders to search the house for rebels and we had to do it. He tried to say something by way of excuse. One of the boys pushed by the girls and opened a closet in the wall. The girl jumped into the door and with tears streaming down her face begged him to stay out. There is nothing in here she said but the wardrobe and relics of my dying mother. She took him by the arm and pushed him away and closed the door. The house was soon crowded with soldiers and the door of the closet opened and examined but we found nothing but dresses and cloaks and bonnets and blankets. I got ashamed and wished that I was out of it. I went back into the big hall and found a bookcase. I stuck Longfellow's *Hiawatha* in my pocket and Ed. Coleman and Elder Harwood took turns with me reading it on our return to Snyder's Bluff.

When I went outside I found several buildings on fire. The orders had been not to set any fires, but nobody cared and nobody would tell. Suddenly a report came in that a body of rebels had been seen by our cavalry some four miles inland. We hurriedly got into line and for two hours marched back through the deepest, darkest forest I ever saw. All at once there came the ring of rifles on every side. The ranks were broken and men supposed to be brave as lions dodged right and left, while others fired their guns out of pure fright with no enemy in sight. It had turned out that we had surprised a company of rebel cavalry who were boiling coffee for an afternoon lunch and after emptying their carbines at our cavalry scouts and giving us a good surprise they retreated in every direction through the woods.

It was lucky for us after all. We had just pulled ourselves together for a forward march when scouts came galloping up with the news that 4,000 rebels under the command of Marmaduke were flanking us on both sides and had already planted cannon on the crossroads between us and the river. In less time than I am telling you we were countermarching at double quick. We made four crossroads to the big plantation and at every one of them we expected to be raked by rebel cannister and grape. Before we reached the last crossroad, shells from our gun boats were screaming over our heads and bursting in our rear, scattering death amongst the rebs as it seemed to us letting us get back into the open cotton field of the big plantation with not a man lost. But it was music to hear those shells ripping through the tree tops on their mission of death. We knew it meant our salvation and death to the rebels.

When we got back to the big plantation we found nearly all the buildings on fire save the mansion alone. The barns, gin house, sawmill, and immense drying sheds were all ablaze sending up columns of black smoke. The cavalry that followed us told us that we had barely crossed the last crossroad when the rebels planted a battery not fifty rods from our line of retreat so as to rake us at the crossing with cannister. There is no doubt our gunboats that kept up a rapid fire over our heads was a mighty lucky thing for us. The rebels had three men to our one and knew every road and vantage point; but for our brass war dogs they would have made it hot for us. We boarded our boats and with one gun boat for convoy, leaving two at the bend for protection to passing vessels, reached our old quarters on the Yazoo yesterday.

Don't forget to send a paper now and then. You are right when you suppose it is hot down there. Dan Hadley and Henry Morse are both on the sick list and about twenty-five others you don't know in the company. I am glad to hear that you have help for harvest. I hope mother won't need to go in the hayfield this summer nor rake up grain. It is too hard work and it don't seem right. I loaned all my stamps and I must hunt one to send this letter. Love to mother and the rest.

Your boy,
Chauncey.

SNYDER'S BLUFF, MISS., JULY 15, 1863.
HD. QUARTERS 25TH VOL.

Dear Brother:

I have for many days thought of writing to you, first because I like you and second because you are not writing to me as often as you ought.

Since the surrender of Vicksburg on the fourth of this month there has been all sorts of rumors as to our future movements. The late battles won by the Army of the Potomac along with the victory over Pemberton here at Vicksburg somehow make us boys feel that the end of the war is near. O, if you could have seen and heard what I have these ten days past. Pemberton had nearly thirty thousand all surrendered to Grant on the 4th of this month. And they were glad to be prisoners and paroled to go to their homes. They cursed the war and called it a nigger war. I heard lots of them say, that had never owned a nigger, that they were fooled and wished they had stayed at home. The bombardment of Vicksburg the night of the surrender was fearful. The clouds above the city looked blood-red as if they were all on fire. The thunder of the cannon for two or three nights and the rumor of surrender kept us awake. We that were rather on the sick list with chills and fever were pretty anxious at the reports that the rebel General Johnston was daily preparing to attack us. Since the surrender the troops by brigades and divisions have gradually withdrawn. All this means that the danger of attack is past.

While I am writing this letter our scouts have brought in word that the rebel General Johnston has been bagged with 65000 troops. Some of the boys are wild over the news, others simply smile and say it's nothing but a false rumor. Whether it is true or false you will know by the papers before this reaches you.

Some of the boys were down to the city of Vicksburg today. They said it was a pretty nice place, but it was badly shot up. Nearly half the town had been burned and the streets were torn up by our shells. It costs twenty dollars in Confederate money to get a meal, and one dollar in U.S. Greenbacks. The darkies were filling up the town and grinning and showing their white teeth at every corner. Grey headed niggers and pretty quadroons begged the soldiers for money and blessed Abraham Lincoln for sending them south to make them free. Most of the boys hate the blacks and say hard things about them. I never can forget what father told me at Mr. Fuller's place when I got in the wagon after that awful good dinner to go to Alma. You remember it brother W. He said if you ever get a chance, my boy, take good aim and shoot twice to free the black while shooting once for the Union.

I don't dare say anything like this to the boys, because they would laugh at me. But I have read enough to know that Phillips was right and Garrison was right and he thought as they did. And I thought for days after going to La Crosse of the tears I saw in his eyes as he asked me always to remember the slave.

Well, brother, to change the subject, have you killed any prairie chickens this summer? It is nearly time for pigeons again. Good Lord, how I hope I can be with you to eat speckled trout and prairie chickens this fall.

I am writing this upon my back. The doctor gave me something for my fever that makes my head whirl. When he came to my tent this morning I asked him if I was very sick. When I told him I was seventeen he said, "you ought to have been thrashed and kept at home two years longer." I told the doctor that he looked sick himself, and he admitted he was not feeling well.

Say, how are the neighbors coming? How does Geo. Cartwright behave? Does he and uncle Ed. cock up twice as much hay as you and father? What does Edward Cass busy himself about? Have he and father got that big field fenced in yet? And Maggie C. is she as pretty and haughty as ever? How does Jim Pierce prosper this summer? Has he commenced that brick house he never tired of telling about? I sometimes wish lightning had struck that man, father then might have got a better farm. Pierce took father in just because he was too honest. Do the cows break in the fields any this summer? Does mother make lots of cheese and butter? Great heavens, what butter and cheese mother could make. When those people from St. Louis came through there and praised mother's bread and butter I thought they were fooling, but now I know they were telling the truth. Well, I have got some soft bread to-day noon! some biscuit I bought of a settler. And I have some butter I paid 50 cents for and some coffee. Don't you think I have a first rate supper? Just like the little boy in the third reader who was happy over his porridge alone when he discovered that everything else of the meal had been stolen.

Love to yourself, father, mother and sister D.

Your brother,
Chauncey.

SNYDER BLUFF, MISS., JULY 19, 1863.
25TH REGT. WIS. VOL. INFT.

Dear Sister:

I got your much valued letter containing your likeness nearly two weeks ago. I was pretty sick at that time with the fever, the Yazoo fever. Since then I have written home. Just two weeks ago I was taken with the chills the day after the fall of Vicksburg. But I ain't alone, there are thousands along this river of death, that's what the boys have named the Yazoo, that are on their backs just like me.

The doctor has knocked the chills for the time at least, though they have made me weak. Dan Hadley and Bill Anderson look in on me once in a while to see that I want for nothing. All the other boys that are well have their patients too. Every fellow has his chum to wait on him. It rained night before last and all day yesterday and there was a hot steam rising from the ground. But it settled the dust and the moving troops don't kick up any dust. We can hear the scream of boats on the Mississippi and

Yazoo night and day. Troops are being shipped up and down the river points fast as boats can get here. Several batteries have passed to-day with six and eight big sleek horses to each gun. The gunners were laughing and calling to one another like a bunch of schoolboys. Moving infantry is constantly in sight. A regiment of cavalry is just now trotting slowly by. Their saber scabbards freshly scoured look bright in the sun and their horses after their long rest are acting pretty wild. I often wish I had got transferred to the cavalry like Ed. Cartwright did at the first. There is a little more danger but you don't have to walk and that saves a soldier a lot.

They are fitting out some hospital boats and after the troops fit for service are transported the sick and convalescent will be taken to northern hospitals. I hear that some three hundred in our regiment are to be put on. I don't know whether I fall within that last or not, but I fear I do.

The doctor says we can't recruit in this hot climate but must get farther north. We are looking for marching orders any day, for some point up the river as far as Memphis, Tenn., or perhaps to Kentucky. Mensus Bump has just been in to see me. He said I made myself sick by eating a whole can of oysters. What he meant was this: The night we went on board for Cypress Bluff we had just had our pay and the boys were hungry for nick nacks. I bought a can of oysters, took it on the boat for fear the boys would steal it from me when I was asleep, ate it all up that night. I knew it was too much but I never thought oysters would hurt a fellow.

Sister D. your picture suits me to a dot. Your face never looked so good to me before, and your letters, say my dear girl, you have a wonderful knack of telling things. Mother always said you were father's girl. I shall be glad when I can do as well as you. You remember Mr. Rosman used to say I was always chipping in when you tried to tell something about catching trout or about father's shooting a deer or a bear. Well, some things you would forget, and I tried to help you out. Say, sister, I haven't forgot how you would scold me for these things when we would be going back over the hill home the next day. Laying here on my back under a tent of thin cotton cloth, under a hot southern sun I can't help thinking, thinking, thinking.

Say, by George, how I wish I could have some of that strawberry shortcake. Land of Goshen, I can taste it now. We have no strawberries but oceans of blackberries. We have plenty of sugar to go with them but no cream.

Well it's getting dull here, most of the troops in sight save our Brigade have gone north or out to follow up the Rebel Johnston's scattered army. It has been so quiet and still since the surrender of Vicksburg it seems dull enough. It is only three miles to the city and the boys that are able run in often as they can get a pass.

The black freedmen are coming in from the country by the thousand and going north to enlist. Several men from our regiment have offered to go as officers in the black regiments. They are doing with the slaves just what General Frémont asked Lincoln to do at the beginning of the war. This is, set the blacks free and make soldiers of them. If you had not sent me stamps, I could not send you this letter. I am glad you like your school. Only look out for the fellow who lives so near. You should go home as often as possible and help mother and take care of sister E. They say she is a dreadful nice girl. Wonder if she isn't a bit like her older brother. Sorry I offended pretty Maggie Cass when I wrote her the black people were human beings and had souls. So she says she won't write me any more? Well unless I run against a rebel bullet or a hard dose of Yazoo fever I'll try and outlive her scorn.

Sam Loomis's company is camping about two miles from here. He comes down once in a while to visit us. He looks pretty thin but his duties as commissary are pretty light so he ought to stand it. I most forgot to tell you Henry Morse and Daniel Hadley have been sick for the last six weeks. They have been getting better. O, how did you pass the 4th of July? I was on picket duty that day though sick enough to be in bed. It's the fashion of soldiers to run on comrades who complain of being sick. They call it playing off. I have noticed that the fellows that do that kind of jibing are infernal cowards themselves. I have learned that the Dutch boys make the bravest soldiers. They don't do any bragging and they are ready for service no matter how dangerous. Is there any one working your eighty this summer? I am thinking what a fine farm my forty and your eighty would make together.

If Myra Amidon ever asks you whether or not I received that letter she and you wrote in company, tell her I did of course and answered it and directed to you. If she wants an answer tell her to write on her own hook and I'll be glad to answer. Tell her I owe her a grudge for beating me at that foot race through the cornfield to the house. My heavens how that girl can run. Myra has the nicest blue eyes I ever saw. How easy it is to write and write of friends and dear ones at home. You will be tired when you read all this, and I must quit. Kiss mother for me and save one for yourself.

Your brother,
Chauncey.

Snyder's Bluff, Miss., July 25, 1863
Hd. Quarters 25th Regt., Wis. Vol.

Dear Mother:

I feel just like writing you to-day. I am sitting in the shade of a big Cypress tree, on the banks of the Yazoo. Looking across the river I can see on some flood trash, two black things looking like aligators. They don't move and I am not sure. There is a pretty spring just below where I sit and a sign over it which says, "Don't drink this water, poison." It is as big as the spring at the head of our coulee and as pure looking. It seems strange that we cannot drink out of the springs here that look just as they do in Wisconsin. Some of the boys don't mind the sign. Some that are burning up with fever and thirst manage to stagger down here and fill up with water and go back to their tents and die. Say mother, what would you think if I should say I have sometimes wished when the fever made me so hot I could hardly stand it that I could go to sleep and never wake up till the war was over. Now this may sound kind of weak for a soldier.

But I am no coward, mother. I don't come from that kind of stock. I remember how you put the gun at the head of your bed when father was gone to Fountain City, ready to use it if Indians should come or wild animals attack the cattle. And father came home and he would pat you on the back and say "You are just the girl for a pioneer's wife." I remember these things mother, and under all circumstances I shall never forget that my father and mother were brave people.

I wrote brother Warren the day before getting your letter so I have delayed answering yours. I am a great deal better from chills and a sort of intermittent fever. I have been taking quinine which seems to have broken the chills. I am thankful it is not that other kind of fever that is killing off the boys so fast. Twenty-three men have lately died out of our regiment. There are only about 100 men out of the regiment fit to do duty.

Thank goodness we are about done with this part of the South. The report now is that our entire Brigade will go to Memphis and on up the Tennessee where a northern soldier can live. Two regiments of our brigade have already left, the Third Minnesota and the Fortieth Iowa. The Twenty-seventh Wisconsin and our regiment will leave soon and then hurrah for a healthier climate. The rebel General Johnston and his Butternut band have skedaddled to parts unknown. Of course you have heard of the retreat of Gens. Lee and Bragg, and of the riot of the mob in New York City and the burning of negro asylums and school houses. That mob uprising looked bad for the North. It was a Democratic crowd in sympathy with the South. Cost what blood, time and treasure it may, the Union will yet win out.

We were paid off the other day, and to my surprise nothing was taken out for extra clothes drawn. Maybe they will take it out later. We got full pay, $26.

This makes twice we have drawn pay at this place. You ask what general it was that ordered that killing retreat, for retreat it was, from Satartia to Haines Bluff? It was General Kimball, a Potomac General, who is now acting General for our corps. We are not in love with him, and some of the boys say he will get shot by his own men the first fight we get into. It is time for roll call and as I am not excused I must quit and go back to camp.

Love to father and the rest,

Your son,
Chauncey

SNYDER'S BLUFF, MISS., JULY 28, 1863.
HD. QUARTERS WIS. REGT.

Dear Mother:

Your last letter at hand. There is no medicine like a letter from home. Let me tell you mother it does a fellow a lot of good. I am glad you are having such success with the bees. It makes my mouth water for biscuit and honey. I wish you would not take so many chances of getting stung. You ought to wear a veil of cheese cloth over you face. Don't think so much of me. I am all right. We have a plenty to eat. By paying a good round price we can get almost anything good to eat. I wish you would think more of yourself. When I see you in my sleep working in the hayfield helping to get up the hay it troubles me. I suppose as you say that help is hard to get and maybe there is no other way. I am careful you may be sure what I eat. Our dainties we get of the sutler, and it is nearly all in cans. I eat a lot of oysters and I find them good for me. That deer that father killed must have come in good play. Don't spoil your relish for it by constantly thinking of me. I told you I am all right. When I get a dish of oysters I always think how fond father is of them.

You say they are going to get rich in Bennet Valley where father bought that forty for me. Well I am happy to know that. It may be they will have use for a part of it when the next recruiting officer comes that way. Nor will he, likely as not, waste his eloquence in trying to coax them to enlist as J. A. Brackett did when I enlisted. He will like as not tell them to furnish so many men or stand a draft.

This war ain't over yet. There may be a lot of money paid out for substitutes yet. Just think of it, they are paying as high as a thousand dollars for substitutes in many of the states. It all means that people are getting tired of the fussy way the war is being carried on. If the slaves had been declared free right at the start, just as father said, and put into the ranks to fight, the war might have ended long ago. I see by the papers there are fifty thousand freedmen under arms and they are doing good service. The poor black devils are fighting for their wives and children, yes and for their lives, while we white cusses are fighting for what Capt. Dorwin calls an idea. I tell the boys right to their face I am in the war for the freedom of the slave. When they talk about the saving of the Union I tell them that is Dutch to me. I am for helping the slaves if the Union goes to smash. Most of the boys have their laugh at me for helping the "Niggers" but Elder Harwood and Ed. Coleman and Julius Parr and Joel Harmon and Chet Ide, the last two of Mondovi, tell me I am right in my argument.

I am sorry father lost that deer. He should take old Prince to help him next time. It is too bad to wound a deer for the wolves to catch and eat up in that way. We have fresh beef all the time since the surrender. These canebrakes are full of half-wild cattle, and they are fat as butter.

I thank brother W. for sending me those stamps. I will send him a book when I get to Memphis. Mother, I wish you would send me a small package of butter by Lieut. McKay, who is home on furlough for thirty days. I like John McKay. He is a good man. He is a good officer and fair to his men. His wife, I think, is in Modena, where he enlisted. You will see a notice of his arrival in the Alma *Journal*. For the can of butter you send I want you to reserve a ten-dollar greenback for your own especial use out of the sum I send you. Good bye, dear mother.

Your boy,
Chauncey.

Cairo, Illinois, to Atlanta, Georgia.
March 13, 1864–November 15, 1864.

THE ATLANTA CAMPAIGN

Decatur, Alabama, May 1, 1864
Co. G., 25th Wis.

Dear Parents:
   The march toward Chattanooga began this morning. The order came last night, after an all day's rain to strike tents this morning and be ready at sunrise to march. This means our entire brigade. The enemy's guns that had been pounding away at us for nearly a week were silenced by our batteries two days ago and since then there has been no excitement till the marching order came last night. Rations for three days were given each man which about filled our haversacks. Then at roll call we were told what was expected of us. That we were to join a large army that Sherman was collecting at Chattanooga and that we were to begin a hundred and fifty mile march toward Chattanooga the next day. The boys cheered and said they were glad to go anywhere for a change. We crossed the Tennessee river on pontoons and marched toward Moresville, our old camp. The mud was from three to six inches deep and fearful sticky. Marched about 12 miles and came into camp just as the sun went below the mountains. Our camp is on the grassy bank of a pretty river. I don't know it's name. It has been hot and muggy and the hard work of plodding thru the mud has tuckered me a little. I have just come from the river where I had a good wash. Lots of the boys threw away their blankets and winter underwear. Dan Hadley, who is cook for our mess of four, has called to supper so I must quit for to-night.
   May 2nd:—The reveille roused us this morning before sunrise and a crowd of negroes that had come into camp to look at the Yankee soldiers began singing some plantation songs for the boys. They have a banjo and I tell you they can play it and dance too. I have washed in the river this morning and while Dan and Obe build the fire, fry the hard tack and sow belly, and boil the coffee I am writing a line or two on this heavy sheet torn from a merchant's ledger in Decatur. It's hard

to get paper to write on. On the other side you will see a list of things sold by the merchant to Bill Parker's nigger George back in 1858. "Nigger George" was a slave.

7 o'clock p. m. We made several halts today to rest but the ground was so wet we couldn't lay down without our rubbers under us. A regiment of cavalry passed us as we halted this forenoon and all seemed to be so jolly I wished for a while I was in the cavalry so I wouldn't blister my feet marching. Came into Huntsville, Alabama, just at sunset, having marched 18 miles. A lot of the boys are crippling around with sore feet. I am washing mine three times a day in cold water which helps them. There is a lot of troops gathered here all destined for Chattanooga. Camp fires are blazing everywhere. Fences, boxes, old buildings and every movable thing is picked up and pulled down to make fires. It looks tough to burn up nice picket fences, but the boys must have fires to cook by.

HD. QUARTERS, 25TH WIS. VOL.
HUNTSVILLE, ALABAMA, MAY 3RD, 1864.

Dear Mother:

I think I sent you my last from this place. I am taking this from some scrawls in my note book. I got a letter from home this morning while waiting for orders to march. Am truly glad to hear that you are out of debt at last. It used to trouble me when I went in the field to hoe corn to think that you was in debt. It made my hoe feel heavy. We are on the march again thru pine forests and over mountains enroute for Chattanooga. Troops are coming in and swelling our force from all directions. We are passed every little while by cavalry on good-feeling horses, prancing along, and by four and six gun batteries, eight big horses to each gun, the cannoneers laughing and talking as they pound along in the cassions. The cannoneers have a snap on the road and today as I limped along on a blistered foot, I wished I could trade places with one of them. But I would rather be in the ranks when the tug of war begins. When it comes long range shooting the boys that man the big guns catch it first. I guess I am satisfied where I am. There is talk that the Johnnies are bound to give us a fight at Chattanooga. We have had a long tedious march today over mountains and thru valleys that were pretty and green and wading creeks over shoe top that didn't really help our sore feet. The streams here are clear and cool and come from springs. No danger of fever from drinking Alabama spring water.

Marched 23 miles today. My feet are not so sore as yesterday. Many of the boys are badly crippled and will have to take the ambulance tomorrow. I am glad I ain't one of them. Some of them are shamming and it puts every honest soldier that complains under suspicion.

Not many minutes after coming into camp every fence and movable thing in sight is pulled down to make the fires. God pity this south land when we are done with it.

May 4th. Struck camp, not tents, this morning, for we had none. The sky all spangled with stars was our only covering last night. I lay with my face to the north and for a long time looking at the only thing I knew— the north star and the big dipper. It seems lower down than in Wisconsin.

At Woodville, 8 miles distant, we took the train for Chattanooga. Our cars were cattle cars. Some of the boys said d— the cattle cars, and some said God be praised for even cattle cars. At 9 p. m. we got under way for Chattanooga. Rushing thru the mountains, rumbling over rivers and gorges that made one's head swim to look down. Some of the tressels were fearful high.

May 5th. Woke up this morning just as the train crossed Tennessee River. I must have been jolted round a good deal as I found myself in the corner of the car some four feet from where I lay down. I was awakened by a lot of the boys singing "When Johnny Comes Marching Home." Max Brill and a Company K man, who had somehow got into our car, was leading the band. Max made the noise and the Co. K man made the music.

Arrived in sight of Chattanooga at 11 a. m. The level plain far as I can see is literally covered with troops. Nothing but tents, tents, tents, by the ten thousand. Music by hundreds of bands is floating and humming in the air. 160 thousand rations were issued this morning to this vast army.

And this was before our division of ten thousand men came in. Got off the cars, cooked our dinner and lay round on our blanket watching the steady tramp of columns going and coming until 6 o'clock. We were suddenly ordered into ranks and marched out 5 miles and camped for the night at the base of Missionary Ridge, where our brave comrades made that heroic charge in 1863. Lookout Mountain, whose summit is swathed in a blue cloud, is about four miles distant from our encampment and about the same from Chattanooga.

May 6th. It was late before we slept last night. There was a constant clatter of cavalry passing, of carbines and swords jangling and of the pounding of gun carriages, over the big rocks that made these roads a terror. The boys think we are close to a fight and there ain't much loud talk. The mail carrier is coming to gather the letters, good bye. Will write again soon. Direct by way of Chattanooga.

Your boy,
Chauncey.

P. S. Direct to 16th Army Corps, via Chattanooga.

ARMY OF THE SOUTHWEST
MAY 10TH, 1864.

Dear Folks at Home:

I send you my diary for three days of hard marching and rather hard fare.

May 6th. We had hardly time to swallow our coffee when we were ordered to fall in and march this morning before daylight. We marched out 12 miles thru the Chickamauga battle ground. For ten miles of the way the woods were scarred and limbed and many trees cut in two by solid shot. All the way little mounds showed where the boys fell and were buried. The battle ground is generally level and covered with timber. The heavy shot has mowed fearful paths on all sides thru the tree tops. Camped a little before sunset at Gordon's Mills. Am sitting with my feet in some spring water writing these notes. Several of the boys are with me bathing their blistered feet.

May 7th. Broke camp and began our march at sunrise thru a rough mountainous country, expecting the enemy to attack any minute. Cannonading is heard on our left. Met a lot of poor whites leaving the country. They are a wretched looking lot. They say we are the first Yanks they ever saw. The horses and cattle and pigs, like the people driving them, are the sorriest things I ever saw. The wagons were driven by the women, and the men, with long-barreled guns and five to ten children, all white haired, followed behind driving the cattle and a sheep or two and sometimes a pig. These were all mountain people, the clay eaters and best shots in the rebel army. Some of the boys asked them what they were fighting for, and they answered, "You Yanks want us to marry our daughters to the niggers." Poor ignorant devils. Marched 18 miles today. Went into camp at sunset—such a sunset! Just such as I have often seen in my Wisconsin home, with the bluff tops all warm and yellow just fading into twilight.

May 8th. Marched but 8 miles today over stony roads and steep mountain sides and crossed many beautiful spring streams. Farms, or plantations as they call them here, look as if they had been prosperous but they are all deserted. The negroes have mostly gone and the whites are in the army.

May 9th. It was no secret that we were close to the enemy eighty thousand strong. Our forward march began early. We made from 8 to 10 miles. The left column of our corps met the enemy and for an hour the cannonade was fierce. The ambulance corps brought back many dead and wounded. The wagon trains, several miles in extent, were halted and packed under cover of several batteries of artillery and a big reserve of infantry. Mounted orderlies were coming and going on fast horses all day long. Nobody knew what the next hour would bring forth. We were ordered to keep our guns in prime condition and our boxes full of bullets.

A great army of infantry lay about us, all waiting like ourselves for the order to march. All of a sudden there came a roll of voices in a mighty shout from the rear. While we were wondering what it meant a troop of cavalry came galloping along headed by the famous cavalry leader, Gen. Kilpatrick. It made the boys feel mighty good to see this daring cavalry leader, who was such a terror to the rebels. He is a little fellow, about 5 feet 5 with brown hair, thin beard and mild gray eyes. He kept touching his hat brim as his mare, all foam, went galloping by.

As the yellow sun went below the Georgia mountains last night, the bands from more than twenty regiments filled the air with their music. I wondered how it would strike the ear of the rebel picket on the mountain side in front of us. I rolled in my blanket, with my clothes on, and tried to sleep. About midnight I was awakened from dreams of home by the rushing cavalry horses and the grinding of artillery wagons. We soon learned that the rebel Gen. Wheeler was making a move to capture our supply trains. The wagons were being hurried to the rear and every surrounding regiment ordered to get in motion and join in the retreat. With the rest of the army we were soon on the counter march, in the darkness, over swollen streams and stumbling over stones we could not see, plunging thru the mud and often entangled in the overhanging limbs. God, what a night and what a morning. Can I ever forget it? No never. The retreat thru the hills of Georgia, following the supply trains of the Union army will long be remembered. I am all right and ready for the fray.—Direct via Chattanooga.

Ever dear parents, Yours,
Chauncey

Sherman's Army, May 10th, 1864.

Dear Parents:

I am writing you again today. I wrote you only day before yesterday but all the boys have the fever, as it looks, of writing letters tonight. Cannons are booming both on the right and on the left, and as our Lieutenant says, things look mighty squally for tomorrow. I can't say that I am a bit nervous, but as the boys say, some of us may be where we can't send letters tomorrow and better send 'em now.

We were up and ready for orders to march early this morning but the order did not come until 9 o'clock. The enemy's shells have been screaming and bursting over head, killing and wounding a lot of men in our division.

Marching out to the front some three miles, and we were nearly all day doing it, so conflicting were the reports of our scouts and couriers as to the location and strength of the enemy.

Finally we came to a halt for the night just as the rain was pouring down in torrents. Everything got soaking wet but our powder. We kept our powder dry. I am afraid you can't read this, my paper is so wet and greasy. In my hurry this morning I put my writing paper in my haversack along with my plate and sow belly.

Night came on at last and with it the hardest storm I ever saw. Our little fly tents let the water thru like sieves. We didn't have any time to pick up brush for a bed and so lay on the ground. Some of the boys said they were laying in the water two inches deep when the sentinels came rushing into camp shouting, "To arms to arms, the rebs are coming." Our camp was in a forest of great pine trees, and I had gone to sleep, as no doubt had the others, while the thunder was crashing around us and the wind and rain was pouring thru the pine tops with an awful roar.

We were already as wet as drowned rats when we sprang out into the open storm, slinging on our cartridge boxes and knapsacks and fastening our dripping blankets to our belts, and pulling down our flimsy fly tents and tying them like belts around us and falling into the retreating column fast as we could. No questions were asked, not a word was said, every fellow for the time was willing to obey orders. The brave boys, who generally knew a lot more than Sherman, didn't say a word last night.

We turned our backs to the enemy and retraced our steps over terrible roads, sometimes in mud and water to our middle. It was pitch dark only as flashes of lightning lit up the struggling mass about us. Stumbling over rocks and roots, many fell full length in the muddy water of the overflowing streams and in the muddy track of the plunging column. We made about four miles and halted near a big corral of supply trains. We were ordered to build fires and dry our blankets. It's pretty hard to tell what Sherman is trying to do. The report is that the rebs are making feints at different points along our lines, trying to break thru, and that Sherman is planning to bag their army.

Our retreat last night looked as if we were the party nearest bagged. But you can't tell. Sherman has an awful army. The line is three columns deep and twenty miles long. That the armies are close together, there is no doubt, as we can hear guns going all night long.

We are hearing good news from the Potomac. The sun is fearfully hot this morning and all hands are trying to dry their soaked clothes.

It is ten o'clock and no orders yet to march. The five or six hundred supply wagons alongside us in a big cornfield, with their four and six mule teams all plastered with mud, show no signs of moving.

Word has just come to be ready to march in fifty minutes. Couriers are galloping up and down the line and the officers are calling out orders to pick up and pack up.

Send me some stamps and direct by way of Chattanooga. In haste. Love to mother, sister and the boys. Will write again the first chance.

Chauncey

CAMP IN THE PINE WOODS, NEAR RESACA,
GEORGIA, MAY 17TH, 1864.

Dear Parents:

I have something to tell you this time. We have been in a big fight and lost near three hundred men, killed, wounded, and prisoners. I am mighty glad to tell you that I am all right. I had several close calls as did all the boys for that matter. We have been under fire and losing men right along for three days. Many of our boys were killed and wounded at long range firing from the rebel fort by shot and shell so far that we could not return it and had to take it. A good part of the time we were supporting batteries that were trying to silence or dismount the big guns on the rebel fort. I want to tell you the Johnnies were all fixed for us. Think of two hundred guns on our side, 12 and 14 pounders, pouring shot and shell fast as men could load and fire into the enemy's fort while two and in some places three, lines of infantry were compelled to stand or lay in front of these batteries, exposed to shot and bursting shell and no chance to shoot back. I don't know where to begin to tell you, nor how to tell you, of the last four days, besides we are under marching orders to be ready to go at a moment's notice, just as we have been night and day for several days. As I write this, cannons are roaring on our left toward Buzzard Roost and no soldier knows what the next hour may bring. I can scarcely keep my eyes open to write, altho it is but ten o'clock in the morning. We have had so little sleep for a week, night or day. On the 12th, word was passed that the rebs had made a stand at Resaca and that the place was fortified and mounted with big cannons and mortars. During the night of the 12th, Sherman planted his batteries on every hill and ridge overlooking the town, and in the morning of the 13th, at day break, both the rebel fort and our brass batteries opened a terrific fire. Our regiment was ordered to take a position in advance of a string of batteries, while another column of infantry filed in front of us.

It was a sight never to be forgotten, to see, as we could from the ridge, column after column of troops, two and three lines deep, forming in battle line away on our left for a mile and a half. Here and there a bursting shell from the fort would throw the lines into confusion killing and wounding scores of men. By the time the smoke cleared up the lines would reform, the dead and wounded would be carried back by the ambulance corps. All that day until night, the big guns on the fort thundered at our batteries on every hill and ridge, on the north and west side. I don't know what our loss was. A shell burst just over us, killing and wounding a number in Co. K., next our Co. A shell burst directly over me, cutting a hole in my blanket and the piece making a hole in the ground within a few inches of my body. The battery, just in our rear, was put out of business for a time by a bursting shell from the fort, dismounting three guns, killing and wounding the gunners, and smashing the gun carriages to splinters. It was a horrible sight to see the poor fellows wounded and mangled. Long before night the valley of the Coosa was thick with smoke so that we could no longer see the belching clouds of smoke sent out from the fort. I see a courier galloping to headquarters. I suppose it means an order to fall in. Will finish my story of the battle Resaca if I live, first chance.

The mail carrier is calling for letters so good bye. Am feeling fine.
Your boy,
Chauncey

CAMP IN THE PINES, GEORGIA.
16TH ARMY CORPS, MAY 18TH, 1864.

Dear Parents:

After we finished breakfast and had strapped on our cartridge belt, our haversack and our knapsack and cleaned and primed muskets and fallen in, an order came to be at ease for an hour or so until a long column of cavalry and artillery, which wanted all the road, could get by. Our foxy old General Sherman was coming another flank move to the right, and the cavalry and artillery were ordered ahead.

There is heavy firing five or six miles on our left and word has just been passing down the line that the rebs at Dalton have made a fierce sortie on our lines at that point. It looks strange to see our troops marching quietly to the right with all this rumpus on the left. But our bully old General knows his business and we feel easy.

I have something more to tell you about Resaca, while we are resting. The evening of the 14th, under cover of the smoke that filled the valley just before sundown, the lines of infantry were advanced nearly a mile toward the town. Our regiment was put on the extreme front. We crossed the Coosa creek or river, about as big as the Elk at Gilmanton, and took up a position in the edge of the woods with a big open plantation or clearing between us and the rebel infantry, lined up in a strip of woods at the edge of this clearing a quarter of a mile from us. The rebels discovered us first and began a terrific fire on us from their cover of brush and logs. Then the order came for us to open fire. There is no use to try to tell you of the excitement, of the cries of the officers, of the whistling of bullets and shells and above all else the roar of guns. Every fellow loaded and fired fast as he could. We were ordered to rest on our knees instead of standing where we could, as at short range firing most of the bullets went high. We had not emptied our boxes before it got dark and we had to aim at the line of fire from the guns of the enemy. After it got quite dark the firing stopped and we went back to the bank of the Coosa and made our coffee, and spreading our ponchos or rubbers on the wet earth lay down on our stomachs with all our belts and belongings fastened to us, and tried to sleep. It was poor sleeping. We thought of the poor fellows who were taking their last sleep and of the many who were suffering from wounds and broken limbs. Long before daylight we were ordered to dig trenches and pile up log barricades on the edge of the open clearing still nearer to the rebel line of defense. There was no warm coffee the morning of the 15th. We lunched on hard-tack and some smoked bacon and ham that our cavalry boys had captured the night before and rationed out during the night.

10 o'clock a. m. We have just had a bugle call to fall in, but after standing in the ranks a half hour, we were ordered again to "grab a root," meaning to rest standing or lying down. I take my pencil and here goes for the rest of my story.

All night long some of the wakeful boys heard officers on the fort swearing and giving orders. Some thought it meant they were moving their big guns or they were planting more big guns. Anyway when the first streak of daylight came both sides opened a hot musketry fire. Both sides were protected behind barricades. We thought it strange that there were so few big guns being used at the fort.

Our batteries, a half mile at our rear, opened up their thunder upon the town with very little reply. By midday the smoke in the valley of the Coosa became so thick we had to shoot by guess. I emptied my cartridge box many times during the day as did the others. I saw men often drop after shooting, but didn't know that it was my bullet that did the work and really hope it was not. But you know that I am a good shot.

During the day we took turns sleeping behind our log barricades. I could sleep but many could not with ten thousand guns roaring in their ears.

Say, do you know that it was my 18th birthday? Shortly after noon one of our cannon shot away the rebel flag on the fort. There must have been twenty thousand Union soldiers see it fall, from the shout that was sent up along our lines. Such a day and such a night. When night set in not a gun replied from the fort. The firing ceased on our side. The night of the 15th we lay upon the bare earth, eating cold scraps such as we had and listening to sounds at the fort we could not understand. In the morning our pickets reported that the high bridge across the Coosa had been burned and the rebel army had retreated. Not a gun was fired in the morning. The fort was silent as the grave. There was a hasty gathering of regiments and forming into column. But I have no more time for details.

There is a roar of big guns on our right and the cavalry and batteries that have been stringing leisurely along, are whipping their horses into a trot. They have orders to hurry up.

Good bye.
Your son,
Chauncey

NEAR LOST MOUNTAIN, GEORGIA,
2ND BRIGADE, 4TH DIVISION,
16TH ARMY CORPS. MAY 20TH, 1864.

Dear Parents:

I have been too busy to think of writing for some days, and if not busy have been sleeping or trying to sleep. We have had ten days and nights of fearful campaigning. The doctors are sending back thousands of men who are sick and dying for want of sleep. There hasn't been a minute of time, night or day, that guns are not heard or that our regiment has not been losing men, and yesterday it all wound up with a most terrible fight at Dallas or Lost Mountain.

I am writing by the light of a rail fire laying on my stomach about 1 o'clock in the morning. Have been on special duty digging trenches and piling up log breastworks in expectation of an attack. This sort of thing has been going on for eight days. One day we would march to the right and the next day to the left. Last week we dug trenches during the day and marched by night, this week we are marching by day and digging nights. The rebel generals keep Sherman guessing most of the time. If we did not have a much bigger army, we would stand a poor show in these mountains. For a week we have been winding round mountains, wading mountain streams and twisting about in great pine woods, falling asleep as we marched and stumbling over roots and stones. Then we would come to a halt to let some cavalry troops get by or some batteries that were badly wanted at the front. Then we would drop down on our faces where we stood and snatch a few minutes' sleep, only to be routed by that awful bugle call to rouse up and march. The fact is, the bugle terrifies us more than rebel bullets. In many places the valleys or gorges in these mountains are so narrow that we have to wade for a long way in the streams that run down them. Of course our feet are always wet, but this water is good to drink and we thank God that we don't suffer from thirst as we did.

Lieutenant McKay has just come round, as he is on duty tonight, and warns me that I better quit my writing and go to bed, so I must leave off telling you of the battle of the Lost Mountain until next letter. I took two or three naps while scribbling this and maybe you can't read it. I am feeling fine. Have had no letter from home lately. Tell Dora to see Miss A. and ask her to write. Direct to Chattanooga, 16th Army Corps.

Goodbye mother and father.

Your loving
Chauncey

40 Miles from Dallas, Georgia,
In the Great Pine Woods,
June 1st, 1864.

Dear Parents:

For three days we have been on special detail duty guarding a supply train of several hundred wagons of hard-tack and ammunition. We came into camp late last night, and while the wagon train has pulled out this morning we are told to be at ease until future orders. I am in the shade of some great pines this morning and I am glad, for the heat of the sun is fearful. With my back against a great yellow pine I am seated to tell you of the fight at Dallas or Lost Mountain. Dallas is a little, sorrowful, humble village of some 600 souls about two miles from a great black forest-covered mound called Lost Mountain.

If I live a hundred years I shall never forget the fearful night of the 29th of May, 1864, when all the earth and sky seemed on fire and in a struggle for life or death. In the space of thirty minutes 2,000 men were killed and three times as many wounded, many of them to die.

Before we reached Dallas on the 27th, we had been told by the natives along the way that a big army of 40,000 men was waiting for us Yanks on Lost Mountain. On account of the heavy timber we were within six or seven miles of the mountain before we saw it. It looked to us like a great big mound two or three miles long covered with a dense forest. We thought of Resaca and of course kept our eyes on the mountain at every opening. We didn't make more than five or six miles that day. A halt would be called every few minutes to let a cavalry regiment cross, going to the right or the left, or a battery, sometimes two or three, would come tearing by, when we would take to the side of the road and drop down on our bellies for a nap till they got by. We camped on the outskirts of Dallas on the night of the 27th between the town and the mountain. There were only a few people left in town and they were packing up and hurrying away in expectation that the town would be burned.

On the morning of the 28th, John W. Christian and I were detailed to go on picket duty. Our beat lay within 80 rods of the rebel breastworks on the side of Lost Mountain. Sharpshooters in the tops of the trees kept pegging away at us for four hours. We changed our position several times but they kept their eyes on us. We were in a cornfield full of rotten stumps. We got behind one of these stumps put up a rubber blanket for a shade and lay clown as close together as we could. They got our range and presently the bullets began to whistle past us, striking the ground but a few feet from us. I said to John, "Let's get out of this." "Wait," he said, "until they come closer." The next moment two shots ripped through the rubber above us, one of them grazing John's breast and tearing a hole in the ground between us. We rolled out of that in a hurry, grabbed our blankets and took a position lower down the hill. John Christian is a dandy boy. He isn't afraid of anything. In the afternoon about 4 o'clock, we were relieved to take a sleep.

As soon as it got dark we were ordered to build breastworks of logs not more than fifty rods from the rebel lines just across a deep gulch from the foot of the mountain. About ten at night we were ordered back to camp for a few hours sleep, and the next morning at three o'clock before daylight, we were in these trenches facing the rebel lines, which were protected like ours. All day long we shot wherever we saw a hand, a head, or puff of smoke, and the rebels did the same. Some times our side would call out to the rebs, asking them to hold up and talk things over. "All right," they would say, and for some time both sides would talk over things about the war, and about their girls, and about exchanging hard-tack for ham, and whiskey for tobacco. Then some voice would call out, "Look out for your life!" and the shooting would begin. Several times during the day both sides would agree to a truce for ten minutes or twenty minutes, and some of the more daring on both sides would meet half way and exchange tobacco for whiskey and sometimes newspapers, sometimes to shake hands merely. Soon as the first fellow got back to his barricade he would call out, "Say pard are you ready?" If the answer came back, "All ready!" at once a dozen guns, perhaps a hundred would answer back the challenge.

About the middle of the afternoon the canteens of my squad, some 30 men, were empty. The orderly called for volunteers to take the canteens and carry them back to the branch some 60 rods and refill them. I was the first man to step out and Jake Bolunger of Alma followed me. Jake and I made the trip all right both coming and going over a ridge in plain view and range of sharpshooters who pelted us with a shower of bullets both ways, Jake fell down on his way out not twenty rods from the trenches. I had got to a stump and made a halt to get my second wind. I called to him. He answered back, "I am all right." The rebel sharpshooters thinking they had killed him stopped shooting at him, when he jumped up and ran over the ridge out of sight. We got back with our canteens of water all safe.

Early in the evening of May 29th after a day of incessant musket firing we were ordered back to camp along with the rest of our division. There had been a rumor that the Johnnies (rebels) were evacuating and still another story that they were concentrating all their cannon along the line of our front and were planning an assault. There was a mystery about it that kept our officers guessing. The thing that looked suspicious to us, if we were to make a flank move, was the increased number of batteries that were lined up along the crest of the ridge just above and behind us. Word was passed along the line that old Leather Breeches, with his eight big brass bulldogs (cannon) had taken a position just in our rear. Leather Breeches had the best battery in the army and every soldier knew that when the old Dutch captain's war dogs barked it meant business. Before the smoke had cleared away, that sent a shell into the rebel ranks, the boys would run up and hug the guns and call them dear girlie.

We were in the edge of a cornfield littered with stumps and stubs. In the three lines lying just in advance of some fifty big guns on the ridge we could see all of our division and part of another. We ate our hard-tack and drank cold water for supper and we lay down for a little rest with all our belts and blankets strapped on. Everything had grown quiet along our front save a few shots from the sharpshooters. On our left there was an occasional boom of cannon some miles off. Yes, and now and then a burst of spiteful musketry close on both our right and left. We were finally lulled into a broken sleep by the music of many regimental bands, which our General had ordered to keep playing. We lay down on the bare earth with everything strapped to us but our guns and the air of "Home Sweet Home" in our ears. It was near 1 o'clock at night. There was no threatening sound save the steady tramp of the 16th army Corps with its infantry and cavalry and batteries moving steadily to the left without any voice of command. Our cat-naps were giving way to sound sleep when, from the forest height of Lost Mountain, there came a chorus of bugle notes that caused 50,000 Union soldiers tired and weary, to spring to their feet. We knew too well that it meant an onslaught of the rebel army. In an instant we were on our feet. The next moment came the command: "Lie down until the enemy shows itself above the crest of the hill." I have no pen to tell you of the awful scenes and sounds of the next three quarters of an hour. How near the rebel infantry came to our lines that night we do not know. The heavens above us seemed to boil with fiery red smoke from ours and the rebel cannons. It must be we were too well prepared. Not a half mile from our right a thousand men were killed in 30 minutes and three thousand were wounded, perhaps most of them mortally. O God, what a night was the night of May the 29th for Sherman's army. It was a night of dazzling, glaring, shrieking sounds. The earth seemed crashing into ten thousand atoms. The sky but an hour ago so pitchy black, seemed boiling with smoke and flame. And the horrid shrieking shot, and bursting shells, then the shouting of commanders and cheering of men, mingled with the sputter of muskets and the roar of batteries, made the world about us seem like a very hell. Just behind our division alone was a solid line of cannon for near a half mile, vomiting fiery streams of shot and shell that came screaming close above our heads. Many of them were so badly timed that they burst above our lines killing and wounding our own men. And for every broadside from our big guns there came an answering roar from the rebel lines. The real death struggle at short range musket firing was a quarter of a mile on the right of our division. The forest there was dense and unbroken. There most of the 4,000 men, who were killed and wounded, fell and all in less than an hour. We talked it all over with the fellows who were in the thick of it next morning. How they were under marching orders to move to the left, how they had quit the trenches under the belief that the rebel army was retreating. Then came those bugle notes which meant a rebel charge and a fight to the finish. They may tell of hell and its awful fires, but the boys who went thru the fight of Dallas with all its scenes, are pretty well prepared for any event this side of eternity. Full of whiskey and gunpowder the rebel ranks charged again and again the Union lines, only to be repulsed again and again with fearful slaughter. They charged with their hats pulled down over their eyes like men who cared only to throw away their lives. With every repulse of the rebels, a cheer of victory came up the Union lines and was borne away in a mighty roar by fifty thousand eager voices on our left. For the rest of the night we slept upon our arms within ear shot of the cries of the wounded and dying, every house in Dallas being pressed into service as a hospital. The cries of the wounded and dying murdered all sleep for me that night and I thought many many times of father's saying: that every life taken by Union or Rebel bullets was a sacrifice to the crime of slavery.

You may have to pay some extra postage on this heavy paper. I am writing on paper torn from some merchant's ledger, picked up in the streets of Dallas. The boys have run out of letter paper and are using any sort of paper.

Orders have been passed along the line to be prepared for a night's march.

I have not had a letter for some days. The report is the railroad in our rear has been cut by a raiding party. If this is so you may not get this letter very soon.

There is a rumor that the rebel army is making another stand at a place called Big Shanty.

Am feeling all right. Love to all.

Chauncey

HEAD QUARTERS FIRST BATTALION
2ND BRIGADE 16TH ARMY CORPS,
CAMP IN THE GEORGIA PINE WOODS.
JUNE 2ND, 1864.

Dear Mother:

I awakened this morning with my face and feet both outside my rubber blanket, washed by the falling rain. I was on duty until 1 o'clock digging trenches and building breastworks. Our division of six regiments is on special duty guarding supply trains of wagons loaded with ammunition and provisions for a hundred thousand men. Since I wrote you last our brigade has moved twice, but not more than two miles each time. The fact is, we move as the rebel army moves. We are on the extreme right of Gen. Sherman's big army, and we have to be wide awake and on the alert for the flankers. Most of us have been wet to the skin night and day for several days. Our worry is to keep our powder dry, for our lives we are ordered to do this. We like the wet better than breathing the thick dust that fills the air from the tramp of so many thousand feet. We don't fear any sudden attack from the rebel's general Hood or Polk en masse, but the bodies of rebel cavalry are hovering round ready to pounce on our provision trains and on their guards any hour of the day or night. This compels us to be always on the move, changing our position. Yesterday a reconnoitering force of the enemy, supported by a battery of artillery came out on a hill a mile and a quarter distant and opened fire upon our lines just in our front. For some moments the sputtering musketry and bursting shells sounded like a general engagement. But soon, to our delight, Leather Breeches, with his war dogs and their cassions drawn by 128 big horses, galloped into position just behind us and with eight big guns opened fire with their ear splitting roar on the rebel battery. It seemed nip and tuck to us fellows, who were waiting with our muskets, as to which would quit first in this duel of big guns. The rebels had fewer cannon, but they were fighting, as their smart leaders told them, for their wives and children. A heavy rain began falling about this time and the rebel cannon ceased firing altogether. As some of the boys say when they run against Leather Breeches, they are "sure up against it." The next morning early a body of our cavalry, sent out to reconnoitre, surprised a company of them playing cards in a log house and captured 40 of them. The boys sent up a wild hurrah when they heard of this. We cannot forget the boast of the South that it would take four "Yanks" to match one Southerner. And do you know, mother, I somehow had the feeling that the South was more than our match man for man, they did so much bragging. But that's their way, besides if they were not fighting to keep us away from their homes we could tell better. The prisoners we talk with, and we see them every day, say we "Yankees" are fighting to free the niggers so they can marry white women. What miserable stories they tell.

It is raining today a slow, drizzling rain. Have just come in from a two hours' stunt on the trenches. The boys who have taken our places are working in a pouring rain and are wet to the hide. They are deepening trenches and piling up musket-proof breastworks, which as Col. Montgomery says: "We may leave the next hour or possibly not for a week." The boys make a joke of their digging by saying there is silver in Georgia and they are mining for it. And then it is taken as a good sign that we are soon to leave entrenchments which it takes a day and a night to build.

I sent you a letter day before yesterday giving an account of our late movements, so I am keeping you well posted.

George Ide, of Mondovi, died yesterday. He had been sick but two days. Poor fellow, what will his parents think? Chet Ide, his uncle, felt very bad. He had been with the company but a short time but the boys will miss him because he was such good company.

A good many of the boys are breaking down for want of sleep. The doctors are sending them back by the hundred to rest and recruit.

Am feeling all right. Hope to get a letter tonight from home.

Your son,
Chauncey

In the Pine Woods, Georgia,
16th Army Corps,
June 6th, 1864.

Dear Parents:

I am off duty and have had six hours of refreshing nap. Henry Morse has just been to see me and asked me to say nothing that will get to his folks about his health. He is bad off with bowel trouble, but he doesn't want his people to know of it. They have cut our rations in half and every fellow is hungry. Every few days our cavalry raiders capture a lot of smoked meat and corn pones, and lots of the boys overeat because it's good, and they are down sick. Henry is one of them. The trouble is, we can't eat here like we can in Wisconsin. If we eat a good fill we are off our feed for a day or two. When our rations are short the boys go to the Quartermaster's and, if they have a dime, fill up on pie and cake, and it's regular poison to them. I dreamed last night about the cheese which you wrote about in the letter I got three days ago. Sure, I would like a taste of it, but, mother, I wish you would stop making cheese with all your other work, it's too much. Mother, I don't remember that I helped you very much in such work, but it seems to me if I was home again I could help you in so many ways that I never thought of before, and I will be home again some day. I am sure we soldiers will have good times again to pay for this. This war will not last always. Gen. Grant is flaxing them in Virginia, and I saw the other day in an Atlanta paper that Gen. Sherman could "outflank Hell," so there is a show that we will outflank Hood and get into Atlanta before long. Let not the people of the North find fault and wonder why we don't press on faster. Great Heavens, think what we have to do. I used to wonder why the Potomac army did not move faster. Then I knew nothing of marching in armies of one or two hundred thousand men. Let people stop and think about these things, then they will be more patient. Let me tell you something about it. Sherman has five army corps of from 15 to 25 thousand men in each corps. Each corps is following in the same direction on parallel roads from 3 to 5 miles apart. Each corps means a string of men, four abreast, of from eight to ten miles long. There is an army of rebels posted on every one of these roads with cannon at every crossroad, cavalry dashing in upon our flanks and sharpshooters picking our men off at every opening where the pine forest comes within a half or quarter of a mile of the road. You can see the time we are having. If one of the corps is stopped by trees fallen across the road so the cannon or the cavalry cannot pass, couriers are sent to stop all the other corps until the way is cleared. All the bridges are burned by the retreating rebels and have to be rebuilt, which causes a delay. Sometimes we use pontoons, boats made of canvas anchored in the rivers with planks stretched from one to the other. Where the roads are obstructed they fall timber on both sides for miles and sharpen the limbs so we can't get thru. A dozen times every day we come to a halt, for what we don't know. It's a safe guess that it's a broken wagon axle, a crippled cannon or a played-out cassion truck. No questions are asked. We are only too glad to fall down on our faces and snatch a few minutes sleep. There are more delays from ammunition and "sow belly" wagons breaking down than from any other one cause. Then the guerrillas are forever attacking our rear guard, and sometimes bodies of men and batteries have to be sent back to help them out. All this means a delay.

Sister Dora wrote that father expected to buy a couple of cows of Mr. Harvey. I think it a good deal as I shall want lot of milk, butter and cheese when I come home, if I do, this winter. Every body thinks the rebellion on its last legs, and that means the end of it when we get into its strongest and last defense, Atlanta.

An orderly has just ridden up to the Brigade Headquarters and, as it may mean something serious, will close for this time. Please send stamps in your next.

Your son,
Chauncey

25TH WIS. VOL. INFT., 16TH ARMY CORPS,
4TH DIVISION, JUNE 11TH TO 14TH.

Dear Mother:

I am no baby but your letters bring tears to my eyes sometimes. You tell me of so many things about home and what you are doing, what Elder Morse and the neighbors at Gilmanton are saying, and about the cows, the pigs and the chickens that I can see them almost as well as though I was there. It is the same old story here. All of the past four days have found us on the line of battle with skirmishers close in front popping away at each other night and day, never stopping for the awful rain that has been falling day and night for two weeks. For days, especially, it has been a steady down-pour of cold rain. We have no tents that will turn anything but dew, and everything that we have, but our powder, is soaking wet. We are in a great flat field and all about us is flooded with water. We have to lay on raes and brush and logs to keep off the wet ground. The rebels are posted on a hill or mountain four miles in front of us. Their signal flags, with which they talk from one army headquarters to another, are plainly seen by us thru the day though we don't read their signals. By night on the distant mountaintops they build fires by which they talk to each other.

Our corps, that is the 16th corps, is about the center of the advancing column, which means a strip of country about 30 miles wide. We are on a railroad running direct to Marietta some 8 miles out. Gen. Hooker is on the right flank and Thomas on the left, and both are closing in toward the center. Kenesaw Mountain fortified with a hundred cannon and looming down upon us stands between us and Marietta. We are so close to Kenesaw on our front that they cannot depress their cannon so as to drop their shells into our ranks. They are trying it with all their might. I am sure there are thousands of boys like myself, half asleep and half awake, who are taking their chance of being blown to pieces. The fellows who are well are passing the time away playing cards in the ditches behind trenches. Now and then a bursting shell spoils the game, mixes the count, and starts a row. By and by peace is declared and the game goes on.

It's a strange life we are leading. While it rains most of the time, there comes a day of sunshine so fearfully hot we keep moving our blankets to keep in the shade of the trees. With the naked eye we are so close to the rebel lines on the top of the mountain that we can see them moving about. We are too far to use our muskets and they are too high to use their cannon on us. Once in a while a shell drops amongst us and then every fellow playing cards or taking a nap gets a move on himself. We don't mind the musket shots ripping thru the tree tops and killing a man now and then, but those shells, when they strike, dig a hole big enough for a cellar and they make the dirt fly. When they fly over your head they make a scream that is terrible to hear.

There was a bunch of us called for a drink the other day at a house where an old lady met us. She looked cross enough when some of the boys sat in her easy chairs. She said we would get a good licking if we ever met the rebel Gen. Johnston. One of the boys asked her why he did not whale us at Dalton, or Tunnel Hill or Resaca. "He would," she said, "if Gen. Sherman and another regiment hadn't outflanked him." There is a fearful roar of cannon on our left at this minute. It must come from our side. I don't understand it because we are at the extreme left of the line of fortifications on Kenesaw. Thank heaven the rebels are not in it with us when it comes to cannon. We have the big guns and can hammer down their lines of defense, and we need them because it's one line of defense after another.

But enough for this time. No letter for some days. Dan Hadley is calling for coffee, but I don't care for any. Have been a bit off my feed for some days. The war will be over some day. Goodbye.

Your son,
Chauncey

CAMP NEAR ACWORTH, GA.
16TH ARMY CORPS. JUNE 19TH, 1864.

Dear Father:

I am writing some of you nearly every day. I don't exactly know why either. One thing that set me to thinking of home was when Henry

Morse came and bid me good-bye. He had been ordered to report to the field hospital. Henry was feeling bad and he looked bad. Say as little about it as you can to his folks. Henry was never tough, he had no endurance. I was sorry to see him go because I don't believe I shall ever see him again.[1]

I have something else to tell you. Yesterday was a mighty eventful day to our brigade. In the morning orders came for three companies of each regiment to get in position and be prepared to charge the rebel lines on the farther side of the plantation bounded on that side as on ours by a heavy forest. In a short time fifteen companies of our brigade were in line, and under cover of a bit of rising ground we advanced to within sixty rods of the rebel earthworks and took a parallel position to them along a washout or gully with a big peach orchard between us and the rebel lines. Here we waited for nearly an hour while sharpshooters in the treetops beyond the peach orchard kept picking off our men. Our orders were to save our ammunition and not to fire a shot. Then came the command to fix bayonets and charge the rebel lines. Then we climbed out of our ditch and made a wild rush for the rebel lines. The air was alive with whizzing bullets and the wild shooting of the enemy tore up the sand and filled our eyes with dirt. We reached the rebel lines without firing a shot, and strange enough we lost but a few men killed and wounded on our side. The retreat of the rebels was complete. Soon after our occupation of the rebel lines, some darkies who had deserted the rebel army came to us and told us how the rebel General Polk had been killed in a log house near our lines. They pointed out the holes made by the twelve-pound shot of our cannon and showed us the blood stains on the logs of the hut.

We can see Kenesaw Mountain in the distance and the rumor is that the rebel army will make a big fight at that point. There is a railroad passing near us that runs into Marietta just beyond Kenesaw Mountain and for some reason Gen. Sherman keeps an engine armored with steel plates running back and forth as near the mountain as he dare. I wouldn't like to be the engineer.

As I write I can hear cannons eight or ten miles on our right and the

---

1. Henry never returned to the regiment. He died in a field hospital and was buried in a plain board box under the solemn pine trees in whose branches every south wind chants a sad requiem above his grave. [*Wisconsin Magazine of History*]

boys say it's "Leather Breeches." They know him by the rattle of his cannon. We had not been an hour in our new camp before we were under marching orders for Kenesaw Mountain.

Will write again soon.

Your son,
Chauncey

HD. QUARTERS, 25TH WIS. VOL. CAMP,
NEAR KENESAW MOUNTAIN, GA.
JUNE 24TH, 1864.

Dear Parents:

Had just nicely finished my notes for yesterday in my diary when we were ordered to fall in for picket duty on the skirmish line. There was no hesitation on the part of any of the boys. They knew well enough what it meant. It was just as if the southern army was invading Buffalo county, not a man of them knowing a foot of the country, yet they were expected by their officers to hold their own against the native inhabitants, who knew every road and bypath and hill and valley. The rebels had their lines already made. Under cover of the night our lines were pushed close to theirs. We made a bargain with them that we would not fire on them if they would not fire on us, and they were as good as their word. It seems too bad that we have to fight men that we like. Now these southern soldiers seem just like our own boys, only they are on the other side. They talk about their people at home, their mothers and fathers and their sweethearts just as we do among ourselves. Both sides did a lot of talking back and forth, but there was no shooting until I came off duty in the morning. The next relief that went on kept up a constant fire all day long. It rained so hard all the forenoon the boys were in the water over their shoe tops in the trenches. This is just about the 99th time it has rained since this campaign commenced, and it's no drizzle drozzle like we have in Wisconsin, but a regular downpour.

June 25th. When the pickets came off the line this morning they had quite a pretty story to tell of how they chummed it with some Louisiana rebs. A company of our Indiana boys met a company of Louisiana rebels half way between the two lines. They stacked arms, shook hands, exchanged papers, swapped tobacco, told each other a lot of things about their feelings and how they wished the war would end so they might go back to their homes and be good friends again, shook hands once more with tears in their eyes as they bid each other goodbye forever, and after calling to each other to be sure that both sides were ready, commenced a furious fire on each other.

Again the report of Gen. Polk's death is confirmed. He was cut in two by a cannon shot not 50 rods from where we charged the rebel lines at Big Shanty. The death of Gen. Polk means that the rebel army is now in command of Gen. Hardee. This means more fighting. Hardee is a hot head and will force the fighting.

The valley between us and Kenesaw Mountain is full of smoke from cannon that have been vomiting their awful fire all day long. We are so close under the mountain they do us very little damage. Our batteries, just in our rear, have been paying them back with interest.

An order has just come that some twenty of our company are to go on picket duty tonight, and I am in that list. I had just put aside my note book when the captain called to me and said I would be excused. I hate to own it but I am very close to the sick list. I am not scared a bit, I am sure I shall be all right soon.

Your boy,
Chauncey

HEAD QUARTERS, 2ND BRIGADE,
16TH ARMY CORPS, NEAR KENESAW MOUNTAIN,
GEORGIA, JULY 4TH, 1864.

Dear Folks at Home:

Many things have happened in this war cursed land since my last letter to you. Only the next day after my last letter of June 28th the rebel army under Gen. Hardee made a fierce attack on our lines on the right. It was unexpected by us. The day had been fearfully hot when just before sunset, when the big guns had stopped their terrible booming, all at once there came up from the right wing a spiteful burst of musketry. It started not a mile from our front and kept getting heavier as it sounded farther away. We had just finished supper, and many of the boys had commenced their card games. Then the boys began to yell, "That's Hardee, the fighting rebel general." The card games stopped and every man was listening. The musketry grew louder until it was one continuous roar. While we were wondering and listening, suddenly couriers from division and corps headquarters mounted on foaming horses came galloping by, carrying orders to brigade and regimental commanders. Then from the left to the right came the rush of cavalry regiments pell mell, many of the boys without their hats or caps, trying to keep up. Then came the word that the fighting Gen. Hardee, with a picked army was assaulting our lines on the right. While we were rapidly forming in rank, leaving everything but our guns and ammunition, battery after battery came pounding by, the drivers on the lead near horse of every pair whipping with all his might. For nearly an hour we waited and listened to the swelling and receding roar of musketry. There was little or no report of cannon. Both sides were afraid that they might kill their own men. In the course of an hour, as twilight came on, the roar of musketry grew gradually less and finally ceased. The next morning we learned that the rebel general Hardee had been fairly whipped and beside losing nearly two thousand men in killed and wounded, our side captured nearly a thousand prisoners.

We are under marching orders to start at any minute. Like myself many boys around me are writing perhaps the last message to father or mother or sweetheart. It's a fearful strain to live such a life and yet the fear of bullets don't bother me half as much as the fear of disease. But strange to think, soldiers never think of dying of disease. Just the same not ten minutes passes during our long encampments, but we hear the muffled funeral drum and the blank musket discharges, above some soldier's grave, who died a victim of southern fever. I must close. Hardee has been thrashed and the orders are that we are to move to the right. The big black cannon on Kenesaw in front of us are strangely silent. It looks as if the rebel army had retreated. Gen. Sherman has outflanked them again. Good bye,

Your son,
Chauncey

HEAD QUARTERS, 2ND BRIGADE.
IN TEN MILES OF ATLANTA, 25TH REGT., WISCONSIN VOL.
JULY 8TH, 1864.

Dear Father:

I have just finished a breakfast of sowbelly, hard-tack and black coffee, yes, and blackberries, all the time waiting and expecting to hear the bugle call to fall in and march to the support of our boys on the extreme right, where the incessant boom of cannon tells us there is a fight on to the death.

We have been hearing for days that the rebs are concentrating their forces at Nickajack, a creek on our extreme right, where they are planning to make a big fight against Sherman's forces.

I don't know what to say about the way we passed the 4th of July in Georgia. I put in a part of the time reading your old letters, and dreaming in a way of home. Rumors a plenty for two or three days had been talked that Sherman had outflanked Hardee and would soon move the entire army upon Atlanta 20 miles to the south.

On the evening of the 2nd of July there came an order to be in readiness to march at a moment's notice. We packed up all our belongings, tents and all else, and sat around or lay upon the ground expecting every moment to be ordered into ranks. For the rest of the night we lay upon our faces and slept. Many times the rattling of the sabers of passing cavalry or the rumbling of artillery with their heavy guns would awaken me. We knew from this that there was a general movement of Sherman's army to the right. Early on the morning of the 3rd of July we became aware from the unusual silence of the rebel guns on Kenesaw, that something new was in the wind. Very soon word was passed along the line that the rebel army had fallen back and was retreating toward Atlanta. Our Gen. Logan with his 15th Corps, who had been on the alert for just this move, made a sudden dash upon the rebels' retreating lines and captured 3,000 prisoners.

On the evening of the third our Brigade, after advancing some miles on the right in the direction of heavy cannonading, went into camp for the night not far in the rear of the battle line, the smoke filling the valley like a fog.

On the morning of the 4th of July, after drawing our allotment of rations of hard-tack, sowbelly and coffee our regiment marched out to the front to the support of a battery of four pieces that were tossing shell into the woods just in front of us. Very soon the order came to erect temporary breastworks of rails and logs along the edge of the woods, where we stood to shield us from the bullets that kept us dodging behind trees. Here we were ordered to lie down, if need be, to keep out of the way of the bullets aimed at the boys on the front line some 40 rods in our front. It was terrible to be sitting and lying down out of the way of the bullets with no chance to shoot back, and we knew that the boys in front of us were being mowed down like grass. We could see the wounded being carried back on stretchers and we knew that the dead were left where they fell. While the roar of musketry went on in our front we lay flat on our bellies while we munched our hard-tack and ate our raw pork, and expecting every minute an order to advance. Suddenly the firing almost ceased, then it burst out again with terrific fury. Then followed a lull in the firing and a moment after there came a mighty shout and we knew the rebels were whipped. I don't know if we had any orders to advance, but the boys all jumped to their feet and rushed over to the firing line. It was something to see the dead and wounded. Many of the boys were crying like children, running back and forth without hats or guns and cursing the rebels for killing their comrades. The whole army seemed to be turned into a mob. I never saw such a mixup. If the rebels had known it they could have slaughtered us like sheep. No time to say more. Love to all.

Your son,
Chauncey

CAMP NEAR ROSSVILLE, GA.,
HEAD QUARTERS, 25TH REGIMENT, WISCONSIN VOL.,
JULY 13TH, 1864.

Dear Folks at Home:

I enclose a lot of leaves torn from my water soaked diary, written morning, noon and night, just as I happened to have time. The pencil marks spread out so much on the damp paper you can't make it all out.

July 9th—After the rebel army retreated last night, and we got into their trenches, we found that they had suffered a bigger loss than our side. Blood stains along the breastworks, the barked trees and plowed earthworks showed the work of the grape and cannister of our batteries, and the knapsacks and guns that were picked up told the story of their loss. They did not have time to carry away all their dead. I stood guard last night for two hours under the shadow of a big tree within 20 feet of a fine looking fellow. He lay stretched out on his back, both arms extending straight out from his body. He was killed by a bayonet or minnie ball thrust thru his heart. His comrades had torn his vest and shirt front open to hunt for the fatal wound. The bars on his sleeve showed that he was a sergeant. His face with the moon shining on it had a ghastly look. A Missouri boy, who stood next to me, took the flap of his coat, after pulling it out from under him, and covered his face.

The Colonel has just called the captains to his tent and of course it means a move. An orderly from brigade or division commander has just handed a bit of paper to the Colonel.

July 10th—12 o'clock noon. We have marched 7 miles this forenoon toward the left wing. Fearful hot and in a cloud of dust that near strangles one. Just as I am writing, far as I can see up and down the road, thousands of men are lying flat on their faces in fence corners under the shade of trees, around buildings and in orchards; some sleeping, all resting or trying to rest. The road is cleared for passing batteries or cavalry.

Just as the bugle blew for the noon halt I went to a near plantation for water or milk. There were a lot of women and children, but no men, save one very old man. The women all seemed to have babies. I suppose their men were in the rebel army. The manners of the boys were a little rough and some of the women looked scared. They threw themselves down on the big broad porch and talked as if they meant to camp for the night. When some of the fellows came to the door as if to go in, a youngish black-eyed girl took a stand square in the door way. Her black eyes looked so hard that Ed. Coleman said he dodged every time she looked at him. One of the boys asked about the road to Marietta. She said it was 9 miles. She had "hearn tell 'twas a good road but she had never been there," though she was born in that neighborhood. Just to be saying something the boys asked a lot of questions about the rebel army. She said we would find out all about it 'fore we got across the Chatahooche river.

July 11th—Yesterday afternoon our march to Marietta was a fearful hot one. Many of the boys were sun struck and were picked up by the ambulances. Soon as we got in town all made a rush that could, to the bakeries, and bought everything in sight. This morning a lot of the fellows have got the Kentucky quickstep to pay for it. Marietta has been a nice town, but is all torn to pieces by the rebel army quartered here during the siege of Kenesaw Mountain, only three miles away. Nobody in sight but women and children and they keep in hiding most of the time. The boys are packing for another hot day's march. Love to all.

Your son,
Chauncey

FIELD HOSPITAL 16TH CORPS,
MARIETTA, GA.
AUG. 4TH, 1864.

Dear Father:

Your awful good wise letter at hand, and one from Dora received today. I am writing this to you and Dora both. I am so glad things are all right in my dear old Wisconsin home. Oh, if you could but see the world as it is going on about us here, how thankful you would be.

This pretty little village and all the country round about has been overrun by both the Rebel and the Union armies. Only the old men and children and the women are left of the people who live here. All the public buildings have been turned into hospitals for our sick and wounded and some of the fields nearby are covered with tents which are fast filling up.

I am glad you are done with your harvest. Talk about soldiers being heroes. If all mothers of soldiers have done as much work in the harvest field as you say mother has done then the mothers are deserving of more praise than the sons. I wish she would not work so hard. She worries so much about me and never thinks of herself. If mother wants to save me from shedding tears she must save herself more.

I am glad you saved the puppy from poison of the rattle snake. It is a wonder as you say that little Eva has not been bitten. You can't be too careful. Yes tell Dora I would like well enough if I could be there to help eat sweet corn and speckled trout, and seems I can almost taste them away down here. It is pretty tough, but if our patience holds out we shall see better days when this campaign ends. If we can take Atlanta, which is 20 miles from here, now the strongest fortified city in the south, we can march to the sea, and then goodbye to the rebellion.

Shall I tell you what is going on at the front, and in hearing distance of six or seven thousand poor devils like myself mostly on their backs, and listening to the boom upon boom of cannon and wondering if it may mean victory or a defeat for Sherman?

Last night I heard such news that I could not sleep, and with the flap of my tent thrown back so my three companions who lay near me could see we watched the flashes of light from our besieging cannon around Atlanta that lit up the darkened sky until after midnight before we went to sleep.

The news that came to me last night made me shed bitter tears. My chum and my next roll companion, and always my next beat comrade, both on picket and guard duty, was killed in the fight at Decatur. He was shot and killed instantly by a volley of rebel shots from the far side of the street during the surprise and retreat of our forces, near where McPherson our best general was killed.

John was one of the best and bravest boys that ever lived. I thought that I had inherited your courage, father, all that any man should have, not to be foolhardy, but John Christian went beyond me. I wrote to you of his daring at Kenesaw Mountain. Poor fellow he did not need to die there, he might have retreated, but he would not and a minnie ball went rushing thru his brain.

The fighting around Atlanta, if we can believe unofficial reports, is of the fiercest kind. And it seems my regiment is in the midst of it rough and tumble. Today we are getting reports of heavy losses. Our Colonel was badly wounded and Lieutenant Colonel taken prisoner. We hear that Colonel Rusk killed two of his captors before surrendering. Several other officers of the 25th were killed and made prisoners, so the report is, but there is nothing as yet official. It seems our brigade repulsed every rebel charge. Our batteries were taken and again retaken. The rebel soldiers it seems were crazed with gunpowder and whiskey given them to make them brave. They drew their caps down over their eyes and rushed upon our batteries to be mowed down with grape and cannister. The rebels were simply crazed. The rebel General Hardee was wounded and taken prisoner and died in our hospital.

Our splendid Gen. McPherson was killed by a scouting party of rebels, his body taken, and later taken by our boys. I hope what is left of our corps after this fight may be sent back to the Mississippi River, and join the main body, as only two divisions of our corps are here, and they are getting whittled down to brigades.

Word has just come that our boys are being driven back from their lines round Atlanta. Nobody believes it.

No more this time. Kiss my dear mother for her boy.

Chauncey

The Atlanta Campaign

MARIETTA, GEORGIA, 4TH DIV. HOS.
AUGUST 20TH, 1864.

Dear Ones at Home:

I have been waiting all this time for something to write about—that is something new to write about. I could tell you of the red sky over Atlanta every night which we boys look at until we fall asleep. It is the light from burning buildings, set on fire by our cannon.

And the rainbow streams of fire that follow the shells from forty or fifty big mortars—night after night, it's the same thing. They say that most of the city is burned and the people are living in holes in the ground.

We hear every day that the city is about to surrender. The city is still publishing its newspapers and making brags about how they are going to trap the Yankees. We don't know how they do it but we find papers from Atlanta laying around every morning.

I went out on the picket line yesterday to get some berries of the freed-men who come as far as the guards and sell their garden stuffs to the Union soldiers. They are stopped from coming within the lines. The negroes are grinning and happy, but the whites who are all women are a sorry looking lot. They have lost all they had and they never had any slaves.

In their heart they hate the Yankee soldiers and they don't know why either. The most they can say when you ask them why their men are fighting the north is that Lincoln wants them to marry the niggers when they are set free.

Most of the whites are just as ignorant as the slaves. You shut your eyes and you cannot tell by their talk which are the blacks.

I have not seen a schoolhouse outside the towns in all the South. The women we have seen in the towns seem to know more. The good widow who has been giving the Iowa boy and myself dinners twice a week is a wise woman and a good one. Of course her heart is with the South but she is so good to us I never think of her being a rebel. My Iowa chum, Geo. Benning, won't go with me any more for dinner, because he says he is so sorry for the woman when she cries as she does when she speaks of her daughter going away with the rebel Lieutenant.

I am writing this by lamp light. Most of my chums are asleep and snoring. The sky is very red over Atlanta 20 miles away, with burning buildings and the big mortars, when a lot of them go off together, make the ground tremble.

Give my regards to Uncle Ed. Cartwright, and love to all at home.

Your boy,
Chauncey

MARIETTA, GEORGIA, 4TH DIV. HOS.
SEPTEMBER 10TH, 1864.

Dear Sister:

Your thrice welcome letter, so long looked for came last night, and the promised $2 came in it. I was really needing the money for little wants. When you offer these Georgians their money they smile sadly and shake their head. Now that Atlanta has fallen into our hands they feel that the South will be whipped and their money will be worthless.

Your letter had a lot of good news and I went over to read it to my foster mother, that is the woman who has given me so many good meals. She sat in a big arm chair on the broad porch knitting some stockings. I sat down on the steps. When I looked up after reading the letter she was crying. She said, "You must have a good sister and how good it is that you boys from the North can get letters from home while our poor boys cannot write letters to their people at home nor receive any." She said, "I have not heard a word from my daughter who went to Atlanta with her sweetheart, nor from my husband for two months. I don't know if they are living or dead." I suppose there are a thousand women in this town who feel just as she does. There seem to be three or more in nearly every house.

I wrote father last week about the surrender of Atlanta. Since then we have had further particulars. The night before, our shells blew up two of their magazines and set fire to the big depot and burned a lot of their cars. For several days before the surrender and even now we can see clouds of smoke hanging over the city. Nearly the entire place is a burning ruin.

It is just two years today since our regiment was mustered into the service. One more year will let us out and less if the talk we hear of the Confederacy having its back broken proves true.

Day after tomorrow will be two months I am in this darned hospital. Expect to go to my regiment in a few days. A lot of the time here I have had the blues and still I am among the lucky ones to get away at all. On the hill the other side the railroad hundreds of poor fellows lie under little mounds newly made. They will never answer to bugle call any more and to them all troubles in this world are over.

Don't send any more money as we are soon to draw pay and I shall have a sum to send home. Everybody that can is going to Atlanta to see the ruins.

The natives are in hopes of finding out something about their men who were in the rebel army. Some of the women are nearly crazy. Everybody rides in box cars or cattle cars. When the cars are full they climb on top.

My stomach is off today on account of eating some sour milk. I got it last night of a colored aunty on the picket line. This morning it was sour. I scalded it but it upset me.

A colored woman just came to the tent with my clothes she has been washing. She had a two-bushel basket full of clothes and carried it on her head. She was a yellow woman and the mother of six children. The three oldest, two girls and one boy, had been sold to a cotton planter in Alabama.

One of the boys asked her if she cared and she replied, "Shua honey I loves my chilen just likes you mammy loves you." I am sure the poor woman's heart was full, for her eyes filled with tears. I thank God along with father and Elder Morse that Lincoln has made them free. She said her children was nearly as white as we, and that three of them had a white father. To think that these slave-holders buy and sell each other's bastard children is horrible. She took us by the hand and bid each of us goodbye and asked God to bless us and our mothers. I see and hear things every day that make me think of *Uncle Tom's Cabin*. Word has come that we are to be ready to go to Atlanta tomorrow or next day. The boys are making a great hurrah about it.

Direct to 25th regiment Wis. Vol. Atlanta Ga. Goodbye dear sister. And as the wretched slave mother said to me, I say to you, God bless you and all the rest.

Your brother,
Chauncey

APPENDIX:
BIOGRAPHICAL SKETCHES

Cooke's letters refer to a number of general officers from both sides as well as to several politicians and other prominent individuals. Nearly all would have been familiar names during the war and are to those familiar with the history of the Civil War. These brief biographical sketches are intended for those who are not.

Braxton Bragg
Confederate

Braxton Bragg was born in North Carolina in 1817 and graduated from West Point in 1837, ranking fifth in the class. He served in the Mexican War and rose to the rank of brevet (temporary) lieutenant colonel before resigning his commission in 1856. He spent the years immediately before the Civil War as a sugar planter in Louisiana and was appointed a brigadier general in the Confederate army in 1861. Bragg had a number of commands in the western theater, none of which were successful, including an offensive into Kentucky in 1862. He was the Confederate commander during the Chattanooga campaign in the fall of 1863. His failure there led to his resignation of command, and he became military adviser to Confederate president Jefferson Davis. He died in 1876.

Ambrose Burnside
Union

Ambrose Burnside was born in Indiana in 1824. He graduated from West Point in 1847 and was commissioned in the artillery. In 1852 he resigned from the army to work on a breech-loading rifle he had developed. His business failed when he was unable to persuade the army to adopt the weapon. He then obtained a position with the Illinois Central Railroad and was its treasurer when the Civil War began.

Burnside received a commission as colonel of a Rhode Island regiment and fought at First Bull Run. Soon after this he was promoted to brigadier general in the Army of the Potomac. In the fall of 1861 and spring of 1862 he conducted a successful campaign along the Carolina coast and was promoted to major general. He was given command of the new 9th Corps, and his unit fought well at Antietam. In November 1862 he replaced McClellan as commander in the eastern theater.

In December 1862 his plan to trap Lee at Fredericksburg failed with heavy casualties, and Burnside was transferred to command the Army of the Ohio. He again enjoyed success, capturing Knoxville and defending it successfully. His command was brought back to Virginia for Grant's spring 1864 offensive against Lee. A court of inquiry found Burnside responsible for the disaster at the Battle of the Crater during the siege of Petersburg, and he resigned from the army in April 1865.

Following the war he served three terms as governor of Rhode Island and was a U.S. senator from that state when he died in 1881.

JEFFERSON DAVIS
President of the Confederate States of America

Jefferson Davis was born in Kentucky in 1808 and moved with his family to Mississippi at a very early age. He graduated from West Point in 1828. He resigned his commission in 1835 and became a planter in Mississippi. He became active in politics and was elected to Congress but resigned to command a regiment during the Mexican War. He distinguished himself during the war and was appointed to fill a vacancy in the U.S. Senate and then elected to a full term in 1848. He served as secretary of war in the Franklin Pierce administration. Davis returned to the Senate in 1856 but resigned in January 1861 when Mississippi seceded from the Union. A month later he was elected president of the newly formed Confederate States of America and served until the end of the Civil War. He died in 1889.

JEFFERSON COLUMBUS DAVIS
Union

Jefferson C. Davis was born in Indiana in 1828. He enlisted in the army as a private and fought in the Mexican War. He received a commission as second lieutenant in the regular army for bravery and was serving as a captain at Fort Sumter when the Civil War began. Indiana's governor appointed Davis colonel of an Indiana regiment and he served in the western theater. In September 1862 he shot Gen. William Nelson dead during an argument in Louisville but was not court-martialed. He served under Sherman through the end of the war and attained the rank of major general. He remained in the army after the war and died, still on active duty, in 1879.

JOHN CHARLES FRÉMONT
Union

John Charles Frémont was born in Georgia in 1813. He attended the College of Charleston and joined the army in 1838 as a second lieutenant in the topographical engineers. He spent much of the next seven years exploring and charting the West, attracting wide public notice and becoming known as "The Pathfinder." At the outbreak of the Mexican War, he seized California for the United States, increasing his popularity nationally. He was court-martialed for refusing to turn over command in California to Gen. Stephen Kearny and resigned from the army. He served briefly in the U.S. Senate and ran for president in 1856 as the first candidate of the newly formed Republican Party. At the beginning of the Civil War he obtained a commission as a major general and had command of the western theater, based in St. Louis. When Frémont ordered the emancipation of slaves in Missouri, Lincoln recalled him to Washington. A long conflict with Lincoln about policy toward slavery led to Frémont's reassignment and eventual resignation. He served as governor of the Arizona Territory after the war and died in 1890.

U. S. Grant
Union

Hiram Ulysses Grant was born in 1822 in Ohio. A clerical error at West Point changed his name to Ulysses Simpson Grant. He graduated from West Point in 1843 and served with distinction in the Mexican War, where he gained valuable experience in the Quartermaster Corps. In 1854 he resigned from the army due more to frustration and loneliness—his wife and children could not be with him while he was stationed in California—than the commonly cited drinking problem. Grant struggled economically while out of the army and was working for his father and younger brother in Galena, Illinois, when the war began. The army rejected his offer to return to service, but the governor of Illinois appointed him colonel of an Illinois unit that he quickly trained. Once back in the army, Grant rose quickly.

In September 1861 he took command of the District of Southeast Missouri with headquarters at Cairo, Illinois. He moved decisively when Confederate forces moved into Kentucky to secure the strategic locations of Paducah and Smithland early that month. His victories at Forts Henry and Donelson in February 1862 not only broke the Confederate defense line in the west but also were the first victories of any scale for Federal forces. He continued his success in the west combining an aggressive style with a sound grasp of the importance of logistics. In March 1864 Congress promoted Grant to lieutenant general, and he took overall command of the Federal army. He accepted Lee's surrender on April 9, 1865. He was the great Union military hero of the Civil War. After the war he served as president from 1869 to 1877. He died in 1885.

Horace Greeley
Newspaper editor

Horace Greeley was born in New Hampshire in 1811 and apprenticed to a newspaper editor when he was fifteen. In 1831 he moved to New York City and worked as a printer, developing political connections with the New York Whig Party. In 1841 Greeley began publishing the *New-York Daily Tribune,* the first Whig daily in the city. The *Tribune* supported a wide array of reforms and was solidly antislavery. Greeley became well known in reform circles and spoke frequently around the country. The *Tribune* and its editor became national figures. He played an important role in the formation of the Republican Party in 1854.

Greeley was inconsistent in his position during the war. At times he urged aggressive action against the South and at other times advocated negotiations. As an opponent of slavery, however, he was consistent. His August 1862 editorial, "The Prayer of Twenty Million," called for Lincoln to order Federal commanders to liberate slaves. He initially opposed Lincoln's reelection but reversed himself a few months before the election.

Greeley remained an influential figure after the war and ran for president in 1872 as the candidate of both the Democratic and Liberal Republican parties. He lost to U. S. Grant by a wide margin and died shortly after the election.

William J. Hardee
Confederate

William Joseph Hardee was born in Georgia in 1815. He graduated from West Point in 1838. The army sent him to Europe in 1840 to study cavalry tactics. He served with distinction in the Mexican War and afterward wrote the War Department's tactical manual, *Rifle and Light Infantry Tactics*. He served as superintendent of West Point from 1856 to 1860. While on leave in the fall and winter of 1860–61, he advised the governors of Florida and Georgia on preparations for secession. When Georgia seceded, he resigned from the U.S. Army and accepted a commission in the Georgia militia; he transferred to the Confederate army in March 1861. Hardee's service in the western theater included the defense of Atlanta. He was with Brig. Gen. Joseph Johnston when he surrendered his force after Appomattox. He died in 1873.

John Bell Hood
Confederate

John Bell Hood was born in Kentucky in 1831. He graduated from West Point in 1853 and served at a number of posts until April 1861. When Kentucky did not secede, Hood joined the Confederate army as a Texan, the state in which he was serving in the U.S. Army. Hood served in the eastern theater through the Battle of Gettysburg. He and his unit were then sent to join Brig. Gen. Braxton Bragg near Chattanooga. He fought the rest of the war in the western theater. While his aggressiveness had been critical to saving the Confederates at the Battle of Antietam, it proved disastrous in the west, especially at Franklin, Tennessee, in November 1864, when his entire army was all but destroyed. Hood was drawn into the Battle of Nashville about two weeks later, which completed the destruction. He died in 1879.

Joseph Hooker
Union

Joseph Hooker was born in Massachusetts in 1814 and graduated from West Point in 1837. He served with distinction in the Mexican War and resigned from the army in 1853. General-in-Chief Winfield Scott blocked his initial attempt to rejoin the army in 1861, but he obtained a commission as a brigadier general soon after. Hooker began the war in the eastern theater, and Lincoln named him commander of the Army of the Potomac—essentially, commander of the eastern theater of the war—in January 1863. Following his defeat by Lee at Chancellorsville, he was replaced by George B. Meade less than a week before the Battle of Gettysburg. Hooker was sent to Chattanooga after the Union defeat at Chickamauga. He never gained the complete trust of General Sherman, who had overall command in the west, and after being passed over for a position he thought he deserved, Hooker went to Chicago and led reserve troops for the balance of the war. He died in 1879.

Joseph Johnston
Confederate

Joseph Johnston was born in Virginia in 1807. He graduated from West Point in 1829, a classmate of Robert E. Lee's. He was the highest-ranking U.S. Army officer to resign to fight for the Confederate States. Johnston served on Winfield Scott's staff during the Mexican War with Lee and a number of other officers who attained prominence later in their careers. He was appointed quartermaster of the army during the Buchanan administration.

He opposed secession until his home state of Virginia seceded. He then resigned from the U.S. Army and was appointed a brigadier general in the Confederate army. He played a key role in the Confederate victory at First Bull Run but felt others received more of the credit. Other perceived slights about which he complained undermined his relationship with President Davis, and in late 1862 he was sent as overall commander to the western theater. He was largely unsuccessful in the west and was relieved of command in July 1864. In 1865 he was in command of Confederate troops in the Carolinas and surrendered to Sherman in late April, ending Confederate operations east of the Mississippi. He died in 1891.

Judson Kilpatrick
Union

Hugh Judson Kilpatrick was born in New Jersey in 1836. He graduated from West Point in 1861 and served in the cavalry in the eastern theater. He was an aggressive commander, known by his troops as "Kill Cavalry," who frequently took heavy casualties. He was a brigadier general by 1863. Sherman personally requested him for the Atlanta campaign in which Kilpatrick commanded the 3rd Cavalry Division of the Army of the Cumberland.

Kilpatrick resigned from the army at the end of the war and served as U.S. minister to Chile, where he died in 1881.

Nathan Kimball
Union

Nathan Kimball was born in Indiana in 1823. He attended what became DePauw University and taught school while studying medicine. He raised a company during the Mexican War and served as its captain and distinguished himself at the Battle of Buena Vista. After the war he returned to Indiana and practiced medicine. After Fort Sumter he raised a regiment, the 14th Indiana, and led it to Virginia as its colonel. After fighting with distinction in western Virginia and the Shenandoah Valley, he was promoted to brigadier general and fought at Antietam and Chancellorsville, where he was seriously wounded. When recovered, he joined Grant's Vicksburg campaign. Following the fall of Vicksburg, Kimball's division operated in Arkansas for a time, and he was in charge of administering the loyalty oath. Frustrated by that process, he asked to be relieved and joined Sherman for the Atlanta campaign. Following the fall of Atlanta, he was sent to Indiana to use his influence to neutralize the growing antiwar movement there. Before the end of 1864 he was back in the western theater serving under Gen. George Thomas, who commended him for bravery during the Battle of Franklin. He served until August 1865 and then returned to Indiana. He was active in Republican Party politics and the Grand Army of the Republic. In 1873 he was appointed to a federal position in Utah, where he lived until his death in 1898.

John A. Logan
Union

John A. Logan was born in Illinois in 1826. He enlisted in the army for the Mexican War but saw no combat action. After the war he attended Louisville University, receiving a law degree in 1851. He entered politics in Illinois, winning a state legislature seat his father had held. Logan was elected to Congress in 1858 and reelected in 1860 as an anti-abolition Democrat. After Fort Sumter, however, he rethought his position and enlisted in the U.S. Army in August 1861 as colonel in an Illinois regiment. He fought under Grant at Belmont, Fort Henry, and Fort Donelson, where he was seriously wounded. He also played an important role in the Vicksburg, Atlanta, and Carolinas campaigns. Logan's career was hurt somewhat by his not being a West Pointer, but he rose to be a corps commander and was the most successful of the Union "political generals" militarily. Logan led the Western Army in the Grand Review in Washington on May 24, 1865.

He took leave to campaign for Lincoln's reelection in 1864 and was a radical Republican following the war, serving in the House and the Senate. He was the Republican candidate for vice president in 1884. Logan was also a highly visible leader of the Grand Army of the Republic in the decades after the war. He died in 1886.

John Sappington Marmaduke
Confederate

John Sappington Marmaduke was born in Missouri in 1833. His father served as governor of the state. After briefly attending Harvard and Yale, he enrolled at West Point and graduated in 1857. He was stationed in New Mexico when the Civil War began and resigned to accept a commission in a pro-Confederate Missouri militia unit. After the Battle of Boonville, Marmaduke accepted a commission in the Confederate army and received regular promotions from lieutenant to major general. He was wounded at Shiloh and after the Confederate withdrawal from Corinth served in the trans-Mississippi theater. He was captured in October 1864 and was a prisoner for the duration of the war.

After the war, Marmaduke was in business in St. Louis and was elected governor of Missouri in 1884. He died in 1887 while serving in that office.

George B. McClellan
Union

George B. McClellan was born in Philadelphia in 1826. He graduated from West Point second in the class of 1846. He served with distinction in the Mexican War, and the army sent him to observe the Crimean War in 1855. Despite his success in the army, McClellan resigned in 1857 to work as an engineer for the Illinois Central Railroad in Chicago, where he met Abraham Lincoln. Here too, McClellan was very successful. Initially appointed major general in charge of Ohio volunteers, he was given a regular army commission and command of the Army of the Ohio in the spring of 1861. After his initial success in western Virginia and the Federal debacle at Bull Run, McClellan assumed overall command of the Federal army. He enjoyed little success against Lee and frustrated Lincoln with his demands for more troops and more time to train them. McClellan also opposed the Emancipation Proclamation when it was first announced. Lincoln relieved him of command in November 1862. He did not receive another assignment and left the army. McClellan ran against Lincoln in the 1864 election as a Democrat. After the war, he was elected governor of New Jersey in 1878 and died in 1885.

John A. McClernand
Union

John A. McClernand was born in Kentucky in 1812 and moved with his family to Illinois at a very early age. In 1836 he entered politics and after several terms in the Illinois legislature was elected to the U.S. House of Representatives as Democrat. He was a close ally of Illinois senator Stephen A. Douglas. Following Lincoln's election and the secession of the first wave of Southern states, McClernand played a key role in the effort to find a compromise and avoid war. After Fort Sumter, however, he supported military action.

Lincoln appointed McClernand a brigadier general because he was a prowar Democrat who would be helpful in recruiting troops and support for the war. McClernand was assigned to the western theater as Grant's second in command at Cairo, Illinois. He distinguished himself at the Battle of Belmont and was promoted to major general after the battles of Fort Henry and Fort Donelson. He also fought well at Shiloh. McClernand had alienated Grant and other fellow officers by often writing to McClellan, the general-in-chief, and other well-connected political friends and by never mentioning other officers or units in his reports. While McClernand managed to gain an independent command in the fall of 1862, he was soon back under Grant's command. His habit of self-promotion led to his removal from command in June 1863 and after a period of inactivity to reassignment west of the Mississippi. He contracted malaria and returned home to recuperate. After the war he practiced law and served for several years as a circuit court judge. He died in 1900.

James B. McPherson
Union

James B. McPherson was born in Ohio in 1828 and graduated first in the class of 1853 at West Point. He served first as an instructor at West Point and then in the Corps of Engineers. He was promoted to captain in August 1861 and assigned to Boston to strengthen the harbor defenses and recruit a regiment of engineers. He contacted Maj. Gen. Henry Halleck, then commander in the western theater, seeking a post closer to the action and was named to Halleck's staff and promoted to lieutenant colonel. Halleck soon assigned him to Grant's staff as chief engineer, and McPherson won Grant's respect at Fort Donelson and distinguished himself at Shiloh. McPherson managed to maintain a positive relationship with both Grant and Halleck. During the Vicksburg campaign, McPherson was a major general, commanding first the Second Division of the Army of the Tennessee and then 17th Corps. His unit held the center of the siege and was the first to enter the city. He then fought at Dalton, Resaca, Dallas, and Kennesaw Mountain during the Atlanta campaign under Sherman. He was killed in action during the Battle of Atlanta in July 1864, the highest-ranking Union officer killed in action during the war.

Milton Montgomery
Union

Milton Montgomery from Sparta, Wisconsin, was the first colonel in command of the 25th Wisconsin Volunteer Infantry when it mustered in at Camp Salomon. During their participation in the Vicksburg campaign, he commanded a brigade of several regiments, known as Montgomery's Brigade. He led the 25th through the Atlanta campaign, fighting with distinction at Resaca and Dallas. In the midst of heavy fighting at Decatur, Georgia, Montgomery was wounded in the arm and captured. He lost his right arm as a result. Montgomery rejoined the 25th in January 1865 and led them during their campaign in South Carolina. He was breveted a brigadier general for his service.

John C. Pemberton
Confederate

John Pemberton was born in Philadelphia in 1814. He graduated from West Point in 1837 and served in the Mexican War. Pemberton's wife was a Virginian, and after Virginia seceded he resigned his commission. He first accepted a commission in the Virginia army, then was commissioned a brigadier general in the Confederate army in June 1861. In October 1862 he was given command of the District of Mississippi. He was unable to defend Vicksburg against Grant's persistent efforts and surrendered the city on July 3, 1863. In his native North he had been viewed as a traitor because he fought for the Confederacy, and after the fall of Vicksburg he was seen in the same light in the South. He was without a command for some time after being paroled. He was with Joseph Johnston as general inspector of artillery and ordnance when he surrendered his army in the Carolinas after Appomattox. He died in 1881.

WENDELL PHILLIPS
Abolitionist

Wendell Phillips was born in Boston in 1811 to a very old and prominent family. After graduation from Harvard he practiced law briefly but emerged as a powerful antislavery advocate in 1837 and devoted the remainder of his life to a variety of reform causes. He was an ally of William Lloyd Garrison's and a frequent contributor to the *Liberator*, Garrison's antislavery weekly. At the 1840 World Anti-Slavery Congress, he was a leader in the effort to allow women to speak. He was among the most visible abolitionists in the decades leading up to the Civil War. He opposed Lincoln for moving too slowly to abolish slavery. After the war, Phillips continued as an advocate of reform, including women's rights, better treatment of Indians and prisoners, and labor reform. He died in 1884.

LEONIDAS POLK
Confederate

Leonidas Polk was born in North Carolina in 1806. In 1827 he graduated from West Point, where he had professed Christianity and was baptized in the chapel. He resigned his commission immediately after graduation and entered a seminary in Alexandria, Virginia. He was ordained an Episcopal priest in 1831 and consecrated bishop of Louisiana in 1841. He was also a sugar planter, owning a large number of slaves. He helped establish the University of the South at Sewanee, Tennessee.

In June 1861, he accepted a commission in the Confederate army as major general and was assigned to defend western Tennessee and the Mississippi River. His seizure of Columbus, Kentucky, ended that state's neutrality. He fought at Belmont, Shiloh, Perryville, Stones River, and Chickamauga. His relationship with Braxton Bragg, his superior, was so poor that he was transferred to Mississippi after Chickamauga when Bragg preferred charges against him for disobeying orders. He was killed at Pine Mountain while doing reconnaissance early in the Atlanta campaign in June 1864.

WILLIAM ROSECRANS
Union

William Rosecrans was born in Ohio in 1819. He was fifth in the West Point class of 1842 and was assigned to the Corps of Engineers. He spent the Mexican War performing engineering duties in the United States. Rosecrans resigned from the army in 1854 to enter business. When the war began, he accepted a position on

McClellan's staff. Within a few months, he had his own command, the 23rd Ohio Infantry. Lincoln commissioned Rosecrans, a prominent Democrat and Roman Catholic, a brigadier general in the regular army at least in part to build support for the war.

Rosecrans fought under McClellan in western Virginia and completed driving Confederate forces out of the region after McClellan left to command the Army of the Potomac. Rosecrans transferred to the western theater and commanded the Army of the Mississippi under Grant's overall command. The two had a falling out after Rosecrans's successful defense of Corinth, Mississippi. He next commanded the Army of the Cumberland against Bragg and enjoyed success until he was defeated at Chickamauga in September 1863. Only the stand that won George Thomas the nickname "The Rock of Chickamauga" prevented total disaster. Rosecrans was relieved of command and held only one other during the war, in Missouri. He resigned from the army in 1867.

He was briefly minister to Mexico before Grant became president and removed him. Rosecrans served in the House of Representatives from 1880 to 1885 and as register of the treasury from 1885 to 1893. He retired to California, where he died in 1898.

Jeremiah M. Rusk
Union

Jeremiah Rusk was born in Ohio in 1830. He moved to Wisconsin in 1853 and pursued a number of occupations. Elected state assemblyman in 1862, he resigned to serve in the 25th Wisconsin, initially as a major. By the end of the war, he was a brevet brigadier general. After the war he became involved in politics again and served in Congress from 1871 to 1877. He was then elected governor of Wisconsin and served three successful terms. Following his terms as governor, he served as secretary of agriculture in the Benjamin Harrison administration from 1889 until his death in 1893.

William T. Sherman
Union

William Tecumseh Sherman was born in Ohio in 1820. He graduated sixth in the class of 1840 at West Point, having lost two places because of the number of demerits he had accumulated. He served mostly in the South before the Mexican War. During the war he served as a recruiting officer in Pittsburgh and in California.

Sherman resigned from the army in 1853 to go into business. He suffered business reversals and had a difficult relationship with his wife, who did not want to leave Ohio. After an effort to rejoin the army failed in 1859, he became president of the Louisiana Military Seminary (now LSU). When Louisiana seceded he left for a position at a bank in St. Louis, but in May he joined the army as inspector general on Winfield Scott's staff.

Sherman soon had a brigade command and fought well at First Bull Run.

Lincoln sent him to Kentucky to serve as second in command to Robert Anderson, the hero of Fort Sumter. When Anderson resigned due to ill heath and exhaustion, Sherman found himself in command. Sherman could not handle the assignment and was soon replaced and sent to Missouri. He did not do well there either and went home to rest. The press, with which he had had conflicts in Kentucky, portrayed him as insane. He returned to duty, training troops in Missouri, most of whom went on to fight with Grant. By April 1862 he was commanding a division under Grant at Shiloh. After a brief term as military governor of Memphis, Sherman reunited with Grant and served well in the Vicksburg campaign. He then helped Grant raise the siege of Chattanooga, and when Grant assumed overall command of the Union army in 1864 Sherman remained in the west. He followed his capture of Atlanta with his March to the Sea during which he implemented his idea of total war. He followed this with an even more destructive campaign through South Carolina. In 1869 he succeeded Grant as general-in-chief of the army. Sherman retired in 1883 and died in 1891.

George H. Thomas
Union

George H. Thomas was born in Virginia in 1816 and graduated from West Point in 1840. He fought in the Mexican War under Zachary Taylor. He compiled a distinguished career after the war, including a term as an instructor at West Point. When Virginia seceded, he decided to remain with the U.S. Army and fight for the Union. Many in his family disowned him for his decision, and some in the North questioned his loyalty. He often served under less competent, but Northern-born, officers.

After a few months in Pennsylvania, Thomas was ordered to Kentucky and spent the rest of the war in the western theater. Thomas planned battles very carefully, led his troops from near the front line, and provided clear, simple orders. He never lost a battle as a commander. His first major action was the Battle of Mill Springs in January 1862, where he routed a Confederate force seeking to move into Kentucky. Thomas's success, combined with Grant's victories at Fort Henry and Fort Donelson the next month, caused the entire Confederate defense line in the west to collapse. With Don Carlos Buell, Thomas repulsed Bragg's invasion of Kentucky at Perryville in October 1862. Passed over in favor of Rosecrans when he replaced Buell, Thomas protected railroads in western Tennessee and Kentucky and trained his troops. When Rosecrans was defeated at Chickamauga, Thomas's stand allowed retreat into Chattanooga and prevented the complete destruction of Rosecrans's army. He became known as the Rock of Chickamauga. In October, Grant gave him command of Chattanooga and ordered him to hold it at all cost until relieved.

Thomas then served under Sherman during the Atlanta campaign and commanded the occupying forces in Atlanta. When John Bell Hood threatened Nashville, Thomas moved quickly to defend it. His troops, directly under Maj. Gen. John Schofield, soundly defeated Hood at Franklin, Tennessee, on November

30, 1864. Thomas waited and prepared. In the Battle of Nashville a little over two weeks later, he destroyed Hood's army and rendered it ineffective for the balance of the war. He was promoted to major general in the regular army. This was Thomas's last action in the war. He remained in the army until his death in 1870.

Lorenzo Thomas
Union

Lorenzo Thomas was born in Delaware in 1804 and graduated from West Point in 1823. He served in the Mexican War but spent much of his career in Washington in the adjutant general's office and as chief of staff to Winfield Scott. He became adjutant general shortly after the outbreak of the Civil War and had a difficult relationship with Secretary of War Edmund Stanton. Thomas spent much of the time after March 1863 in the field dealing with Federal efforts to recruit African American troops. He became ensnared in the conflict between President Johnson and the Radical Republicans and retired from the army under pressure in 1869. He died in 1875.

Joseph Wheeler
Confederate

Fightin' Joe Wheeler was born in Georgia in 1836 but was educated in Connecticut. He graduated from West Point in 1859. Wheeler resigned his commission in 1861 and joined the Confederate army. He attracted the attention of Braxton Bragg and was promoted to colonel. Wheeler was the most skilled of all Civil War officers in using cavalry to screen advances and protect retreats, a talent he first showed at Shiloh. He fought in some two hundred engagements and had sixteen horses killed beneath him in the western theater. Following the war he was briefly in prison but after his release served fifteen years in Congress. He was commissioned a brigadier general of volunteers during the Spanish-American War and distinguished himself in combat. In 1900 he was given a brigadier's commission in the regular army. He died in 1906.

www.ingramcontent.com/pod-product-compliance
Lightning Source LLC
Chambersburg PA
CBHW070952180426
43194CB00042B/2361